Arthur Rimbaud

Titles in the series Critical Lives present the work of leading cultural figures of the modern period. Each book explores the life of the artist, writer, philosopher or architect in question and relates it to their major works.

In the same series

Antonin Artaud *David A. Shafer*
Roland Barthes *Andy Stafford*
Georges Bataille *Stuart Kendall*
Charles Baudelaire *Rosemary Lloyd*
Simone de Beauvoir *Ursula Tidd*
Samuel Beckett *Andrew Gibson*
Walter Benjamin *Esther Leslie*
John Berger *Andy Merrifield*
Leonard Bernstein *Paul R. Laird*
Joseph Beuys *Claudia Mesch*
Jorge Luis Borges *Jason Wilson*
Constantin Brancusi *Sanda Miller*
Bertolt Brecht *Philip Glahn*
Charles Bukowski *David Stephen Calonne*
Mikhail Bulgakov *J.A.E. Curtis*
William S. Burroughs *Phil Baker*
John Cage *Rob Haskins*
Albert Camus *Edward J. Hughes*
Fidel Castro *Nick Caistor*
Paul Cézanne *Jon Kear*
Coco Chanel *Linda Simon*
Noam Chomsky *Wolfgang B. Sperlich*
Jean Cocteau *James S. Williams*
Salvador Dalí *Mary Ann Caws*
Guy Debord *Andy Merrifield*
Claude Debussy *David J. Code*
Gilles Deleuze *Frida Beckman*
Fyodor Dostoevsky *Robert Bird*
Marcel Duchamp *Caroline Cros*
Sergei Eisenstein *Mike O'Mahony*
William Faulkner *Kirk Curnutt*
Gustave Flaubert *Anne Green*
Michel Foucault *David Macey*
Mahatma Gandhi *Douglas Allen*
Jean Genet *Stephen Barber*
Allen Ginsberg *Steve Finbow*
Günter Grass *Julian Preece*
Ernest Hemingway *Verna Kale*
Derek Jarman *Michael Charlesworth*
Alfred Jarry *Jill Fell*
James Joyce *Andrew Gibson*
Carl Jung *Paul Bishop*

Franz Kafka *Sander L. Gilman*
Frida Kahlo *Gannit Ankori*
Søren Kierkegaard *Alastair Hannay*
Yves Klein *Nuit Banai*
Arthur Koestler *Edward Saunders*
Akira Kurosawa *Peter Wild*
Lenin *Lars T. Lih*
Pierre Loti *Richard M. Berrong*
Jean-François Lyotard *Kiff Bamford*
Stéphane Mallarmé *Roger Pearson*
Gabriel García Márquez *Stephen M. Hart*
Karl Marx *Paul Thomas*
Henry Miller *David Stephen Calonne*
Herman Melville *Kevin J. Hayes*
Yukio Mishima *Damian Flanagan*
Eadweard Muybridge *Marta Braun*
Vladimir Nabokov *Barbara Wyllie*
Pablo Neruda *Dominic Moran*
Georgia O'Keeffe *Nancy J. Scott*
Octavio Paz *Nick Caistor*
Pablo Picasso *Mary Ann Caws*
Edgar Allan Poe *Kevin J. Hayes*
Ezra Pound *Alec Marsh*
Marcel Proust *Adam Watt*
Arthur Rimbaud *Seth Whidden*
John Ruskin *Andrew Ballantyne*
Jean-Paul Sartre *Andrew Leak*
Erik Satie *Mary E. Davis*
Arthur Schopenhauer *Peter B. Lewis*
Adam Smith *Jonathan Conlin*
Susan Sontag *Jerome Boyd Maunsell*
Gertrude Stein *Lucy Daniel*
Igor Stravinsky *Jonathan Cross*
Pyotr Tchaikovsky *Philip Ross Bullock*
Leon Trotsky *Paul Le Blanc*
Mark Twain *Kevin J. Hayes*
Richard Wagner *Raymond Furness*
Simone Weil *Palle Yourgrau*
Tennessee Williams *Paul Ibell*
Ludwig Wittgenstein *Edward Kanterian*
Virginia Woolf *Ira Nadel*
Frank Lloyd Wright *Robert McCarter*

Arthur Rimbaud

Seth Whidden

REAKTION BOOKS

In memory of Ross Chambers, Jean-Jacques Lefrère and Michael Pakenham

Published by Reaktion Books Ltd
Unit 32, Waterside
44–48 Wharf Road
London N1 7UX, UK
www.reaktionbooks.co.uk

First published 2018
Copyright © Seth Whidden 2018

Printed and bound in Great Britain by Bell & Bain, Glasgow

A catalogue record for this book is available from the British Library

ISBN 978 1 78023 980 4

Contents

Note on References and Translations 7

Introduction 9

1 Walls 13

2 Fields 40

3 Capital 61

4 Cities 95

5 Wounds 118

6 Worlds 143

7 Afterlives 177

References 193

Bibliography 199

Acknowledgements 202

Photo Acknowledgements 204

Note on References and Translations

References to Rimbaud's work are indicated in the text, from either of the two editions indicated below. For the sake of legibility I have adopted abbreviations for the following publications:

Corr. Paul Verlaine, *Correspondance générale*, vol. 1: *1857–1885*, ed. Michael Pakenham (Paris, 2005)

JJL Jean-Jacques Lefrère, *Arthur Rimbaud* (Paris, 2001)

OC Arthur Rimbaud, *Œuvres complètes*, ed. André Guyaux and Aurélia Cervoni (Paris, 2009)

OC1 Arthur Rimbaud, *Œuvres complètes*, vol. 1: *Poésies*, ed. Steve Murphy (Paris, 1999)

OPC Paul Verlaine, *Œuvres en prose complètes*, ed. Jacques Borel (Paris, 1972)

'Sensation', 'My Bohemian Fantasy', 'Vénus Anadyomène', 'Sonnet to an Asshole', 'Vowels', 'Seapiece', 'Movement', 'Departure' and 'City', and excerpts from selected poetry and prose by Rimbaud, translated by Wallace Fowlie, from *Rimbaud: Complete Works, Selected Letters: A Bilingual Edition*, © 1966, 2005 by The University of Chicago. All rights reserved.

All other translations are my own.

Paul Verlaine, Arthur Rimbaud smoking a pipe, 1872.

Introduction

Arthur Rimbaud was born in 1854 in Charleville, today called
Charleville-Mézières, a comfortable and quiet town northeast of
Reims and near the Belgian border. It is perhaps appropriate that
Rimbaud's story begins, as it does for many of us, in the classroom.
Before he was a poet, before he wrote a single verse of poetry, he
was one of the most brilliant students his school had ever seen:
winning every competition the school could organize, never hiding
his air of superiority. Part *enfant prodigue*, part *enfant terrible*, having
quickly conquered his lessons, he moved on to the world of French
poetry. As he had done with the masters he had studied, Rimbaud
continued to plunder from the past, take the pieces apart and put
it all back together again, having made it all his own.

Such was the case with the pastoral landscape that surrounded
him: long a fertile ground for Romanticism, it quickly became trite
in the eyes of the young poet already looking beyond its horizons.
From his vantage point walking along the hill that overlooks
Charleville, Rimbaud was looking past. The reigning poetic
movement of the day made the transition from that hill to Paris
seamless: the poets in Paris had adopted as their home Mount
Parnassus, that great mountain from mythology. Having bested
his classmates and fellow townsfolk, Rimbaud had nothing left
to prove and no reason to stay in Charleville. In the hope that
publishing with the Parnassians would provide the escape he
sought, he sent some of his earliest verses to established poets

who were in a position to help him and ventured to Paris, one foot tentatively (and half-heartedly) in Parnassian poetry, the other ready to set down somewhere else. (Unsuccessful, he quickly changed his mind about the Parnassians and pushed his own poetry beyond their Neoclassicism.)

The tumult of 1870–71 brought ground-shaking moments to Rimbaud and to the whole of French history; the capitulation in Sedan and the subsequent loss of the Franco-Prussian War led to the fall of the Second Empire, the Siege of Paris and the Paris Commune. France's Second Empire and Napoleon III were humiliated, and the Prussian siege of Paris created exciting, revolutionary times for young Frenchmen. Their political landscape was upended; in its wake anything seemed possible. Take one young and brash poetic genius, add daily political events that offer new ways of looking at social and cultural space, and stir: in May 1871 Rimbaud sits down and writes two letters – one to his former teacher Georges Izambard, the other to the poet and editor Paul Demeny – in which he spells out the poetic project that will wreak havoc on French poetry. In the letters, Rimbaud first rips apart what he calls insipid, subjective poetry, and proposes in its place objective poetry: with a more detached world view and a greater emphasis on objects themselves. His famous declaration 'Je est un autre' (I is someone else) dissociates the person who writes the poem from the lyric subject – the 'je' – on the page. This notion was not entirely revolutionary in 1871 – Théophile Gautier had already hinted at it some 35 years earlier in the preface to his *Mademoiselle de Maupin* – but Rimbaud was the first, and certainly the most brazen, to develop a full poetic project around this notion of de-subjectified poetry. The other catchphrase that is often quoted from these two letters, 'le dérèglement de *tous les sens*', comes from the declaration that 'the Poet makes himself a *Seer* by a long, gigantic and rational *derangement of all the senses*'. Rimbaud's project involves the deliberate and calculated approach to this undoing – the French word *dérèglement* speaks to the undoing of rules, *règles* – rather than a blanket refusal of poetic authority out of simple adolescent rage. Only a brilliant former student such as Rimbaud, having mastered centuries of verse before he turned seventeen, could revolutionize French poetry so astutely, in order to improve upon it so irrevocably.

He then wrote to Paul Verlaine, a fellow poet ten years his senior, in September 1871, and explained that he had great poetry to write but that he needed to be in Paris to make it happen. The letter and the poems that he enclosed were convincing enough, and Verlaine responded by inviting the young poet to Paris. Thus began a turbulent relationship between the two poets that crossed boundaries both social (marital fidelity, taboos regarding homosexuality) and national (the two were together in France, England, Belgium and Germany). During their time together – stories about which are corroborated by personal correspondence, first-hand accounts from friends and acquaintances, police reports and medical examinations – Verlaine wrote what is arguably his best poetry, and Rimbaud's poems were, in turn, influenced by those of his partner. And then, almost as quickly as it started, the two poets parted ways: after Verlaine shot Rimbaud in the wrist in a Brussels hotel in July 1873, Rimbaud returned to his family's farm outside Charleville and finished writing *Une saison en enfer*, dated April–August 1873 and published the same year. Not including his academic prizes and some other poems that he was successful in placing in small regional publications, it is the only literary work Rimbaud himself published. He stopped writing poetry no later than 1875, when he was 21, and left Europe in 1878. After some peripatetic travelling he lived in Africa as a trader, explorer and gun-runner until his health forced him to return to Marseille, where he died in 1891, at the age of 37. His writings during the last twelve years of his life – letters home and some geographic exploration – only accentuate Rimbaud's definitive departure from poetry and Europe.

What makes Rimbaud's poetry important, and what makes his story so compelling that it needs to be told? Perhaps it is because his poetry of rebellion and revolt, about love and boundaries and walking away from it all, has so much to tell us, at so many ages: not only the teenagers who see themselves in him and who wish to be able to reject authority with similar flair, but all of us who were once teenagers, too. Rimbaud's story is about the brazenness of youth; almost all of his poems were written between the ages of fifteen and twenty. In that short time, and at that young age, he took centuries-old traditions of French versification – rules governing everything from rhyme schemes to syllable counts – and destroyed them. Thematically, Rimbaud's poems combine sensuality with pastoral, parody, political satire, fable, eroticism and mystery. Formally, he wrote in all three recognizable forms of French poetry – verse, prose and free verse – and his free verse happens to be the first two free-verse poems ever written in French. His earliest verse poems present recognizable themes, formal attributes and rhythms; some of the prose poems from the collection called *Illuminations* are so hermetic that one critic famously decided that their main purpose (if not their only one) was their very illegibility. In these poems, Rimbaud does more than merely invite us into his world, though: he dares us to make it our own, in texts that resist whatever attempts we might make. He famously ends 'H' by teasing us, as in a riddle: 'trouvez Hortense' (find Hortense). His poem 'Parade' ends with the line 'J'ai seul la clef de cette parade sauvage' (I alone have the key of this wild circus). Rimbaud's range and depth are infinite, and we readers are constantly challenged to meet him halfway, all the while knowing that halfway to infinity is just as hard to reach as infinity itself.

1

Walls

At the centre of Charleville-Mézières sits the place Ducale, built from 1612 to 1628. The Duke who gave his name to the city's main square was Charles de Gonzague, the Duke of Nevers and of Rethel, and nephew of Henri IV. Charles had been appointed governor of the Champagne region by Henri III in 1589; taking the governor's name, the city of Charleville was founded in 1606 on his birthday, 6 May. Much of the architecture of Charles' seventeenth-century city remains unchanged today; for the last four hundred years, each of the four roads leading out of the central square has been adorned with identically roofed and corniced structures, amplifying the effect of *lignes de fuite*, or vanishing points. Being led away in all directions is fitting, for it was from the place Ducale – from the city's heart – and more generally from Charleville, that Arthur Rimbaud would so often try to make himself vanish. The place Ducale is equally notable for its being based on Paris's place des Vosges, itself begun in 1606 and inaugurated in 1612: Louis Métezeau designed the place des Vosges, while his brother Clément was in charge of the copy in the Ardennes. (The place des Vosges is also where Victor Hugo lived from 1832 to 1848, now the site of the Maison de Victor Hugo museum; echoes between the two poets start early.) Imitating the brickwork, symmetry, uniformity and repetition in Paris, the place Ducale is a less impressive version of its older, metropolitan cousin; the centre of the provincial city seems to be looking over its own shoulder. More locally in the Ardennes region, Charleville was nothing like its counterpart across the river, the medieval city of Mézières. Founded some six hundred years earlier, it was important not only for its administrative status as prefecture but for its strategic position on the Meuse river, with its citadel and layers of fortifications that bear witness to its historic importance like growth rings on a tree. By contrast, Charleville was the new neighbour, with no strategic prominence or particularly strong cultural or historical identity, instead offering iron foundries, manufacturing, and new housing and comfort to the inactive soldiers who liked to stroll idly along the Mézières ramparts. Being in Charleville's place Ducale was thus being in a centre of productivity, purpose and activity, and also being in an echo of another place: a reference to an original to which the city's very walls refer. Is it any wonder, then, that so much of Arthur Rimbaud's early years are, like the place Ducale, focused on going somewhere else? If the notion of flight is indeed particularly useful in understanding Rimbaud's poems, it seems that there are two kinds: sometimes it is clearly Paris that he has in his sights; at others, there is flight not in any particular direction but simply anywhere, as long as it is far from Charleville. Charles Baudelaire captured this sentiment perfectly in his prose poem 'Any Where Out of the World'. That he chose English for his title, infusing the gesture with the unfamiliarity of the foreign, signals the many frontiers that such a flight seeks to cross. We can almost imagine the impish, adolescent Rimbaud increasingly impatient and responsive to the last words of Baudelaire's poem: 'Enfin, mon âme fait explosion, et sagement elle me crie: "N'importe où! n'importe où! pourvu que ce soit hors de ce monde!"' (And finally, my soul explodes, and wisely it yells to me, 'Anywhere! Anywhere! As long as it is out of this world!').

Baudelaire's poetic call to flight was published in September 1867. Rimbaud wrote his first poem (from the manuscripts that have been found, anyway) a year later, on 6 November 1868; he had just turned fourteen. This Latin poem's very title, '*Ver erat . . .*' (It was

Place Ducale, Charleville, *c.* 1860.

springtime . . .), suggests auspicious new beginnings and creates
the space for the opportunism of the younger generation eagerly
awaiting its chance: 'It was springtime [. . .] I seized the moment.
I went to the happy countrysides, leaving all memories behind
me. Far from study and freed from all concerns, I could feel sweet
joys reviving my exhausted mind' (*oc*, 5). Despite the seemingly
infinite rural stretches beyond Charleville, they are insufficient
for the young mind searching for more: 'My young heart sought
more than vain strolls through the countryside; it held much higher
aspirations! I do not know what divine inspiration gave wings to my
exalted faculties. As if stupefied, I remained silent, my eyes lost in
contemplation. I felt a true love for nature on fire rising in me.'

His exalted faculties were already pushing the young poet to look
beyond the limitations of his physical environment. The boy shared
with his three siblings both the surrounding classical symmetry
of the place Ducale and the controlling grip of his mother, the

former Vitalie Cuif, who watched over him in a stern manner from the moment of his birth on 20 October 1854. Perhaps the only surprising aspect of the relationship between the adolescent poet and his mother is not its negativity, but rather the sheer documentation of that negativity: he referred to her as 'la bouche d'ombre' (the mouth of darkness; the phrase is borrowed from one of Victor Hugo's poems in *Les Contemplations* of 1856), he begged his former teacher to help soften her hardened heart, he said that she was as inflexible as 73 administrations with lead helmets, and he once described his despair at being stuck at home by writing, '"la Mother" has put me in a sad hole.'[1] For her part, the devout Mme Rimbaud was oppressively controlling: watching over Arthur's schoolwork, following his every move. Who was fighting the losing battle of instilling order and respect against the powerful forces of adolescent rebellion? An overprotective and even tyrannical parent, or a cautious, respectable mother – more or less upstanding bourgeois woman (with social pretensions) whose soldier husband very clearly had abandoned them, leaving her to call herself Widow Rimbaud? The truth doubtless lies somewhere in the middle, especially since later in life the dutiful son would write to his family incessantly and return to convalesce either to Charleville or to the family farm nearby at Roche; and the tone of his adult correspondence suggests that he grew if not to love, then at least to respect this woman who had worked hard to keep things together while raising four children by herself.

If she was alone, it was because the poet's father, career soldier Frédéric Rimbaud, was most often stationed far from Charleville; his few military leaves and returns home provided as many new branches on the family tree, each visit coinciding with the conception of a new child. While the young Arthur makes no mention of his father – who after being sent to Lauterbourg in 1860 would never again return to Charleville – whatever influence may have existed between them was passed down, not surprisingly, through books. During his eight years stationed in Algeria, Capitaine Rimbaud learned to read and write Arabic fluently; much later, while Arthur was living in Africa, he wrote home and asked for several of his father's old Arabic books, which contained jokes, puns, songs and other material that would help him learn the language.

If he would later pick up Arabic easily, it is in part because from his earliest schooldays Rimbaud had a gift for languages, excelling in Latin and Greek throughout his studies. He was not just any student, though; by all accounts, Rimbaud was a once-in-a-lifetime prodigy who devoured literature and quickly surpassed the masters he was studying. After being taught at home by Mme Rimbaud during his early childhood, he was enrolled at the Institut Rossat in October 1861. With his mother pushing him incessantly and looking over his shoulder – literally, for she would walk Arthur and his older brother Frédéric home from school every day until they were teenagers – in the three years he would spend at Rossat he received over a dozen prizes in a variety of subjects: Latin, French, history, geography and classical recitation. His mother moved him to the Collège de Charleville in the spring of 1865, and he continued at a blistering pace, completing three years' worth of schooling in a year and a half. Along the way, he won just about every academic prize the school had to offer, and his earliest poems, written in Latin or in French, were the results of *concours* or competitions organized by the school. It was at this time that Arthur and Frédéric took their first communion. Theirs was a typical sibling relationship, with high and low points and differing political perspectives (during the Franco-Prussian War, Frédéric's enlistment in the army ran counter to Arthur's anti-imperial rhetoric) and intellectual potential (years later Arthur would write to his mother, 'I would find it quite embarrassing, for example, if people knew that I had a bird-brain like that for a brother. It's not much of a surprise, since it's Frédéric: he's a complete idiot, we've always known it to be true, and we always marvelled at the thickness of his skull'; *oc*, 553). Five years after their communion, Arthur would return to the duty and piety of his youth – with a clear sense of the anguish that it caused – in his poem entitled, appropriately enough, 'Les Premières Communions' (First Communion; *oc*, 139–48).

It was at the end of his year in *seconde* when then fourteen-year-old Rimbaud made a name for himself by winning eight first prizes (he had won four the year before): in Latin verse, *version latine* (translating Latin into French), Latin narration, *version grecque* (translating Greek into French), history, geography, recitation and religion. When he won two regional school competitions for poems composed in Latin, the winning poems appeared in local newspapers. He was more than a whizz-kid, though: he was truly an *enfant terrible*, a whizz-kid with an attitude. His final school prize gives us a glimpse into his brio. Given the assignment of translating part of Lucretius' *De natura rerum* (On the Nature of Things), Rimbaud was inspired by the recently published translation of the same by René François Armand Prudhomme, *dit* Sully Prudhomme (who in 1901 would be the first author to receive the Nobel Prize in literature). Perhaps 'inspired' is a bit of an understatement; Prudhomme's translation would have long since been relegated to the dustbins of history were it not for the fact that the fifteen-year-old Rimbaud not only copied but *corrected* the first 26 lines of Prudhomme's work. The plagiarism went unnoticed, and Rimbaud's prize-winning verses were published in April 1870 under the title 'Invocation à Vénus' (*oc*, 19–20). A notebook of sixteen pages – untitled but commonly referred to by their first word, 'Conspecto', or as the 'Cahier des dix ans', even though the author was probably not ten but eleven years old at the time – similarly attests to Rimbaud's unique ability to draw on encyclopaedic knowledge, make starting points vanish, and irreverently go off on his own: written in French and in Latin, the *cahier* includes maxims, essays,

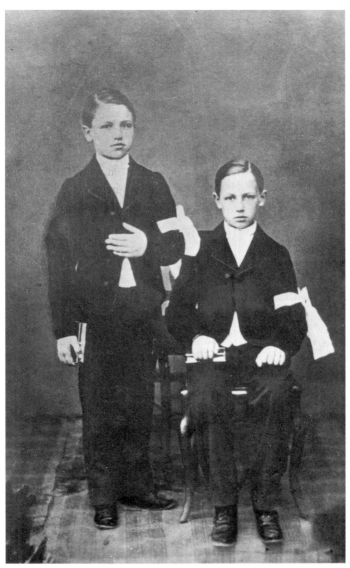

Arthur (seated) and Frédéric Rimbaud, at their first Holy Communion.

Edmond Dubois-Crancé, *Le Vieux moulin* (The Old Mill), 1747–1814.

translations, scribbles, calculations and drawings, and evokes Pliny, Herodotus, Cicero, Seneca, Diodorus Siculus and Phaedrus.

By the spring of 1870, Mme Rimbaud and her children were living in an apartment facing the Meuse and almost directly across from the *vieux moulin*, the seventeenth-century mill that today houses the city's Musée Rimbaud. From this vantage point Arthur and Frédéric had an easy walk to school, and with their younger sisters, Vitalie and Isabelle, they could see the boatyard across the river with the wooded Mont Olympe hovering behind it: echoes of mythology visible and yet – since even once the hill is climbed one has only a view of Charleville to show for it – real grandeur was still very much out of arm's reach. It was from the top of Mount Olympe that young Arthur would write his first verses in French, and the first that he submitted for publication: the poem 'Les Étrennes des orphelins' (The Orphans' New Year's Gifts; *oc*, 15–18), published in the national magazine *La Revue pour tous* when he was just sixteen. The long poem was actually shortened by a third in response to a request for concision by the editor published in the 26 December 1869 issue. Rimbaud assented, acting quickly, and the poem appeared in print the following week, on 2 January 1870:

> *La chambre est pleine d'ombre; on entend vaguement*
> *De deux enfants le triste et doux chuchotement.*
> *Leur front se penche, encore, alourdi par le rêve,*
> *Sous le long rideau blanc qui tremble et se soulève . . .*
> *– Au dehors les oiseaux se rapprochent frileux;*
> *Leur aile s'engourdit sous le ton gris des cieux;*
> *Et la nouvelle Année, à la suite brumeuse,*
> *Laissant traîner les plis de sa robe neigeuse,*
> *Sourit avec des pleurs, et chante en grelottant . . .* (ll. 1–9)

The room is full of darkness; indistinctly you hear / The sad soft whispering of two children. / Their heads lean down, still, heavy with dreams, / Under the long white [bed] curtain which trembles and rises . . . / – Outside birds feeling the cold crowd together; / Their wings are numbed under the grey colour of the skies; / And the New Year, with her train of fog, / Dragging the folds of her snowy robe, / Smiles through her tears, and, while shivering, sings . . .

Amid the quiet awakening of the new year, the orphans are aware of what they lack:

> *On sent, dans tout cela, qu'il manque quelque chose . . .*
> *– Il n'est donc point de mère à ces petits enfants,*
> *De mère au frais sourire, aux regards triomphants?*
> *[. . .]*
> *– Le rêve maternel, c'est le tiède tapis,*
> *C'est le nid cotonneux où les enfants tapis,*
> *Comme de beaux oiseaux que balancent les branches,*

Dorment leur doux sommeil plein de visions blanches!
– Et là, – c'est comme un nid sans plumes, sans chaleur,
Où les petits ont froid, ne dorment pas, ont peur;
Un nid que doit avoir glacé la bise amère . . . (ll. 20–22, 29–36)

You feel, in all this, that something is missing . . . / – Is there then no mother for these small children, / No mother with a fresh smile and triumphant glances? [. . .] – A mother's dream is the warm blanket, / The downy nest where children, huddled / Like beautiful birds rocked by the branches, / Sleep their sweet sleep full of white visions! / – And here – it is like a nest without feathers, without warmth, / Where the children are cold and do not sleep and are afraid; / A nest the bitter wind must have frozen . . .

In Rimbaud's version of the well-trodden theme of orphans and their concomitant feelings of abandonment and neglect, the confinement of the four walls contributes to the poem's despair almost as much as the absence of the maternal. But the children's sadness gives way to nature's gifts – left as if by a fairy – as the warmth of splendour fills the void and replaces the shivering cold:

La nature s'éveille et de rayons s'enivre . . .
La terre, demi-nue, heureuse de revivre,
A des frissons de joie aux baisers du soleil . . .
Et dans le vieux logis tout est tiède et vermeil:
Les sombres vêtements ne jonchent plus la terre,
La bise sous le seuil a fini par se taire . . .
On dirait qu'une fée a passé dans cela! . . .
– Les enfants, tout joyeux, ont jeté deux cris . . . Là,
Près du lit maternel, sous un beau rayon rose,
Là, sur le grand tapis, resplendit quelque chose . . .
Ce sont des médaillons argentés, noirs et blancs,

De la nacre et du jais aux reflets scintillants;
Des petits cadres noirs, des couronnes de verre,
Ayant trois mots gravés en or: 'À NOTRE MÈRE!'
. . . . (ll. 91–105)

Nature awakens and is drunk with the rays of light . . . / The
earth, half-bare, happy to come alive again, / Stirs with joy under
the kisses of the sun . . . / And in the old house everything is
warm and red: / The black clothes are no longer spread over the
floor, / The wind has at least quieted down under the door . . .
/ You could say that a fairy had passed through the scene! . . .
/ – The children, very happy, uttered two cries . . . Here, / Near
the mother's bed, under a beautiful rose-coloured ray, / Here on
the big rug, something shines . . . / They are silver medallions,
black and white, / Mother-of-pearl and jet with glittering lights;
/ Small black frames, glass wreaths, / With three words engraved
in gold: 'TO OUR MOTHER!'

In addition to interior scenes and the mother–child relationship,
Rimbaud's early poems also draw heavily on the open spaces of
nature as sources of warmth, wonder and escape: here, through
the 'rose-coloured ray' and the 'glittering lights', objects increase
in value through their interaction with nature. Whether just
across the Meuse river or at the vanishing point so longed for,
nature is the place of exile, peace, wandering, freedom, and the
kind of heightened awareness of the senses that can only be
felt beyond the walls of one's own existence. Such is the case in
'Sensation', which the sixteen-year-old Rimbaud sent to Théophile
de Banville. Already the author of a half-dozen volumes of poetry,
Banville was one of the most accomplished and recognized
practitioners of Parnassian poetry – the mid-century's leading
poetic style, characterized by Neoclassical references and respect
for the classical tenets of French versification. Initially called Les

Bénédict Masson, *Théodore de Banville*, 1862.

Impassibles, the Parnassians eschewed Romanticism's effusive expressions of emotion and rejected the movement's late turn towards socially useful poetry. Adopting *l'art pour l'art* (art for art's sake) as their unwritten mantra, they turned away from their modern moment in favour of images of beauty that had stood the test of time, hence the profusion of references to statues (beauty chiselled into marble) and tales from antiquity. Rather than forming a literary movement or school, this loose trend took shape in three volumes published by the Parisian editor Alphonse Lemerre, at whose shop in the passage Choiseul the poets would regularly gather. The first volume of *Le Parnasse contemporain: recueil de vers nouveaux* (The Contemporary Parnassus: Collection of New Verses) was published in 1866, in eighteen instalments from March to June and then as a standalone volume in October.

In May 1870 Rimbaud sent Banville the poems 'Sensation', 'Ophélie' and '*Credo in unam*' ('I Believe in One', later entitled 'Soleil et chair', or 'Sun and Flesh') and asked that they be included in the next series of *Le Parnasse contemporain*. The second collection was already underway, its first instalments having begun in October of the previous year.[2] The first of the three poems traces a trajectory through the pastoral: the external voyage turned inward, a full activation of the senses giving way to emotions that words cannot express:

> *Par les beaux soirs d'été, j'irai dans les sentiers,*
> *Picoté par les blés, fouler l'herbe menue:*
> *Rêveur, j'en sentirai la fraîcheur à mes pieds:*
> *Je laisserai le vent baigner ma tête nue . . .*

> *Je ne parlerai pas, je ne penserai rien . . .*
> *Mais un amour immense entrera dans mon âme:*
> *Et j'irai loin, bien loin, comme un bohémien,*
> *Par la Nature, – heureux comme avec une femme!*

In the warm summer evenings, I will go along the paths, / And walk over the short grass, as I am pricked by the wheat: / Daydreaming I will feel the coolness on my feet. / I will let the wind bathe my bare head . . . // I will not speak, I will have no thoughts . . . / But immense love will enter into my soul; / And I will go far, far off, like a gypsy, / Through the countryside – joyous as if with a woman!

'Sensation' seems to offer another echo of Baudelaire's directive 'Any Where Out of the World': Rimbaud's poetic subject qualifies his travels in every way, except where he is going. What matters most is evident via repetition: 'loin, bien loin', the distance relative to here. The very regular cadence of the start of the poem is interrupted with the rhyme between 'rien' (l. 5) and 'bohémien' (l. 7), since the first word is pronounced with synaeresis – in which two vowels are counted as one syllable – and the latter pronounced with diaeresis, splitting the last four letters into two syllables ('bo-hé-mi-en'): in both cases in order to maintain the standard twelve beats of these classical alexandrine verses.[3] This pairing of entities with a slight yet important rhythmic difference is a telling example of Rimbaud pushing back against the basic rules governing French poetry. That he dares to do so in a poem sent to Banville – who was well known as a staunch proponent of classical French versification and who would soon publish *Petit traité de poésie française* (1872), a master stroke of poetic codification that would become standard reading in French schools – offers a glimpse into the kind of brio that would soon become Rimbaud's calling card.

And yet, once Rimbaud is beyond the city walls, even nature fails to offer a solution, as we see in another of the poems sent to Banville, '*Credo in unam*' (the Latin title 'I believe in one' is borrowed from the Apostles' Creed):

> *– Pourquoi l'azur muet et l'espace insondable?*
> *Pourquoi les astres d'or fourmillant comme un sable?*
> *Si l'on montait toujours, que verrait-on là-haut?*
> *[. . .]*
> *Nous ne pouvons savoir! – Nous sommes accablés*
> *D'un manteau d'ignorance et d'étroites chimères!*
> *Singes d'hommes tombés de la vulve des mères,*
> *Notre pâle raison nous cache l'infini!*
> *Nous voulons regarder: – le Doute nous punit!*

Le doute, morne oiseau, nous frappe de son aile . . .
– Et l'horizon s'enfuit d'une fuite éternelle! . . .
(*oc*, 43–4; ll. 89–91, 104–10)

– Why the silent sky and the unfathomable space? / Why the
golden stars swarming like sand? / If one mounted forever, what
would one see up there? [. . .] We cannot know! – We are weighed
down / Under a cloak of ignorance and narrow chimeras! / Apes
of men, fallen from our mothers' wombs, / Our pale reason hides
the infinite from us! / We try to see: – and Doubt punishes us!
/ Doubt, gloomy bird, strikes us with its wing . . . / – And the
horizon rushes off in an eternal flight! . . .

Much less than a refuge, not only is nature not the answer, it is a
series of unanswerable questions to which we simply do not have
the key. What could possibly be worse for the young poet seeking
his own flight than the realization that the horizon that he seeks –
beyond which lies his salvation – is never there, that it is behind
a moving target that he will never reach?

Another reason that made Charleville unbearable was its
provincial mindset, evident in 'À la musique' (*oc*, 94–5). The poem's
stated location of 'place de la Gare' brings readers ever so close to
trains leading out of the city, and on one of the manuscripts the
phrase 'tous les jeudis soirs' (every Thursday evening) underlines
the oppressive monotony of the scene:

Sur la place taillée en mesquines pelouses,
Square où tout est correct, les arbres et les fleurs,
Tous les bourgeois poussifs qu'étranglent les chaleurs
Portent, les jeudis soirs, leurs bêtises jalouses.

– L'orchestre militaire, au milieu du jardin,
Balance ses schakos dans la 'Valse des fifres':

– Autour, aux premiers rangs, parade le gandin,
Le notaire pend à ses breloques à chiffres:

Des rentiers à lorgnons soulignent tous les couacs:
Les gros bureaux bouffis traînent leurs grosses dames
Auprès desquelles vont, officieux cornacs,
Celles dont les volants ont des airs de réclames;

Sur les bancs verts, des clubs d'épiciers retraités
Qui tisonnent le sable avec leur canne à pomme,
Fort sérieusement discutent des traités,
Puis prisent en argent, et reprennent: 'En somme!...'

Épatant sur un banc les rondeurs de ses reins,
Un bourgeois à boutons clairs, bedaine flamande,
Savoure son onnaing d'où le tabac par brins
Déborde – vous savez, c'est de la contrebande; –

Le long des gazons verts ricanent les voyous;
Et, rendus amoureux par le chant des trombones,
Très naïfs, et fumant des roses, les pioupious
Caressent les bébés pour enjôler les bonnes ... (ll. 1–24)

On the square, cut up into measly plots of grass, / The square where everything is right, trees and flowers, / All the wheezy bourgeois, choked by the heat, / Bring, Thursday evenings, their jealous stupidities. // – The military band, in the middle of the garden, / Swing their shakos in the *Waltz of the Fifes*: / – Around them, in the first rows, struts the dandy; / The notary hangs from his monogrammed watch-charm: // Men of independent means in pince-nez point out all the false notes: / Men from huge desks, bloated, drag their fat wives / Near whom, like busy elephant keepers, walk / Women whose flounces resemble

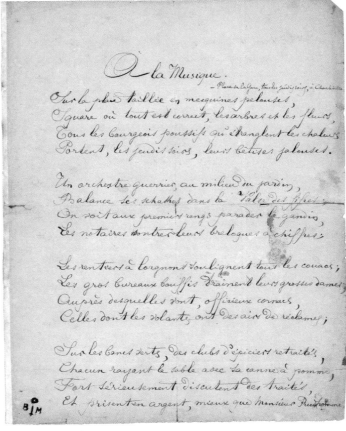

Arthur Rimbaud, 'À la musique', manuscript.

public announcements; // On the green benches, clubs of retired grocers / Who poke the sand with their knobbed canes, / Very seriously discuss treaties, / Then take snuff from silver boxes, and continue: 'In short! . . .' // Spreading over his bench the roundness of his buttocks, / A bourgeois with bright buttons, a Flemish paunch, / Savours his Onnaing pipe, from which tobacco in shreds / Overflows – you know, it is contraband; / – // Along the green grass loafers sneer at everyone; / And, made amorous by the song of the trombones, / Very naive, and smoking pinks, young soldiers / Pat the babies to entice the nurses . . .

If there ever were a poetics of bourgeois suffocation, this one would be it. (Honourable mention goes to 'Les Reparties de Nina' (Nina's Replies; *oc*, 71–4), in which a male protagonist courts his beloved for over a hundred verses, only to receive the shortest of replies: '– Et mon bureau?' (And my office?): her only interests are wealth and status.) The rigid precision and order of the city squares and the military instruments and music are as much anathema to Rimbaud as the city residents' contact with nature is to them. Heat chokes instead of providing warmth. Plots of grass in the city space are chopped up to serve an urban purpose, defined by the foot and carriage traffic and the modern industry that cut through them. Instead of touching the earth with their fingertips, residents poke at sand with canes; 'canne à pomme' refers to a cane with a knobbed handle (rather than a curved one), but it is also a way of distorting nature by drawing the word 'apple' far from its natural state, like the snuff: nature manipulated for man's creature comforts. The city/nature divide extends to their backsides, for they likewise keep their distance by sitting not on the grass, but on stand-ins for nature: benches painted green. And that's just the flora; this 'garden' (by now the sarcasm is clear) is full of equally mocked fauna, as they strut, swing, pontificate and prance about with all the grace that puffed-up, self-important types can muster. That the women are compared to elephant keepers says it all.

Amid this symphony of small-town banality, though, a new voice is about to emerge – specifically, in the poem's final three stanzas:

– Moi, je suis, débraillé comme un étudiant,
Sous les marronniers verts les alertes fillettes:
Elles le savent bien; et tournent en riant,
Vers moi, leurs yeux tout pleins de choses indiscrètes.

Je ne dis pas un mot: je regarde toujours
La chair de leurs cous blancs brodés de mèches folles:
Je suis, sous le corsage et les frêles atours,
Le dos divin après la courbe des épaules.

J'ai bientôt déniché la bottine, le bas . . .
– Je reconstruis les corps, brûlé de belles fièvres.
Elles me trouvent drôle et se parlent tout bas . . .
– Et je sens des baisers qui me viennent aux lèvres . . . (ll. 25–36)

– Dressed as badly as a student, I follow, / Under the green chestnut trees, the lively girls: / They know it, and turn while laughing, / Towards me, their eyes all full of indiscreet things. // I do not say a word: I keep looking / At the flash of their white necks embroidered with stray locks: / I follow, under the bodice and the scanty clothes, / The divine back below the curve of the shoulders. // Soon I have revealed the boot, the stocking . . . / – Burning with fine fevers, I reconstruct the bodies. / They find me silly and speak together in low voices . . . / – And I feel the kisses that come to my lips . . .

As Rimbaud's teacher would later explain, the poem had originally ended with the line 'Et mes désirs brutaux s'accrochent à leurs lèvres' (And my brutal desires cling to their lips). He claimed to have convinced his student to change what – according to the teacher – amounted to the tone of an excessively blustery and stupid heartbreaker, in conflict with the modest, tentative schoolboy of the rest of the poem. Whether because of this somewhat apocryphal story or not, it was Rimbaud who ultimately chose to end the poem with the poetic subject receiving the physical contact instead of initiating it. Many of his actions are subtle: remaining silent, watching, not acting out on the fevers coursing through him. Unlike in the Parnassian aesthetic, here the muse is not a statue but the girls whose bodies the poet virtually and voyeuristically reconstitutes through an active gaze. As we follow his gaze, we see that the subject is defined by the very act of following: repeated in lines 25 and 31 is the homograph 'Je suis', the first-person form of both the verbs *suivre* (to follow) and *être* (to be). While semantically it makes sense that he follows the lively girls and, later, a divine backside, the repetition provides an additional insistence on the *cogito* and supports the passivity of the thinking subject, whose very nature is also inherently related to the act of following others. In some respects he could scarcely do more while still in a poetic universe 'where everything is right'. This poem's greatest irony of all, however, is that Rimbaud would get the last laugh: today his gaze continues to be central to the place de la Gare thanks to his bust that sits there, allowing him to keep looking at passers-by and all the trains that take people far from Charleville.[4]

The physical walls of Charleville and the lines that traced its manicured city squares were equally present in the building blocks of French poetry – granite that Rimbaud made malleable through his own form of poetic alchemy. (According to legend, he also literally wrote on the city, carving either 'Merde à Dieu' or 'Mort à Dieu' into a garden bench.) Even before he sent booby-trapped missives to Banville, asking (and daring) him to publish them, Rimbaud began the subversion of poetic rules in his earliest verses; in 'Les Étrennes des orphelins', for example, the line 'Ah! Quel beau matin que ce matin des étrennes!' (Ah! What a beautiful morning, this New Year's morning!) throws a poisoned dart into the heart of the twelve-beat alexandrine line – the break or caesura that

Bust of Arthur Rimbaud, Rimbaud Museum, Charleville.

traditionally marks the moment of pause between two symmetrical halves (traditional for all verses of more than eight syllables). Instead, the word 'que' here begins a clause that straddles the divide – 'Ah! Quel beau matin que [+] ce matin des étrennes' – and disobeys the rules of classical French poetry by sitting rhythmically in the first half but belonging semantically and syntactically to the second.

Starting in January 1870, the young prodigy studied rhetoric with a new teacher to the Collège de Charleville, Georges Izambard. It did not take long for Izambard's presence to make itself felt: in early May – when her son was sending poems to established poets

Portrait of Georges Izambard.

in Paris, trying to get something started – Mme Rimbaud wrote to the new teacher and implored him to stop putting into the hands of her impressionable son the kinds of texts that he was encouraging his pupils to read. As much as she claimed to appreciate all that he was doing for her son, if there was one thing that she could not accept it was reading books like the one he had given her son a few days earlier (at first she had thought that Arthur had taken it up without his teacher knowing it): 'it would be certainly dangerous,' she explained, 'to permit him to pursue such readings.' The offensive title? *Les Misérables* by a certain 'Victor Hugot' (*sic*). Upon its publication, the novel had been pilloried by the Catholic press for being seditious and profane, and Mme Rimbaud called Hugo an 'enemy of religion' when Izambard went to meet with her in an attempt to clear the air – and also to correct her, since the text he had given his pupil was actually *Notre-Dame de Paris*. Rather than a mutual understanding, the teacher went away with a heightened appreciation for his pupil because of the tyranny of 'la Mother' and the moral distress that he witnessed.

The fact that Hugo was also the most famous political opponent of the Second Empire and Napoleon III made the literary recommendation all the more daring. And yet, Rimbaud hardly needed much encouragement, as he was already more than capable of coming up with his own authorial voice. It is about this time, mid-1870, that the fifteen-year-old wrote the erotic and anti-clerical story 'Un cœur sous une soutane: Intimités d'un séminariste' (A Heart under a Cassock: Confidences of a Seminarian), which first bore the subtitle 'Roman' (Novel), which Rimbaud crossed out and changed to 'Nouvelle' (Short Story). Editions of Rimbaud's work often group this story with other prose works from his schooldays: 'Le Soleil était encore chaud [. . .]' (The Sun was Still Warm), 'Invocation à Venus' and 'Charles d'Orléans à Louis XI'.[5]

Not surprisingly, Rimbaud read both Hugo novels and many of his poems; a year later, while saying that he had his copy of Hugo's poetry collection *Les Châtiments* right in front of him, he would praise *Les Misérables* by calling it 'un vrai *poème*'. Despite this enthusiasm, Hugo would hold a place in Rimbaud's literary heart that was not unlike that of Banville, or even Sully Prudhomme for that matter: a brief period of sincere respect and appreciation quickly replaced with varying degrees of imitation, insults, parody or satire. After being an important intertextual source for poems including 'Le Forgeron' (The Blacksmith) and 'Qu'est-ce pour nous, mon cœur . . .' (What does it matter for us, my heart), Hugo, who allegedly proclaimed Rimbaud a 'child Shakespeare' after meeting him, would later be the object of Rimbaud's satirical poem 'L'Homme juste' (The Just Man). Nor would Banville be spared such treatment, in a poem that some have thought to be Rimbaud's parody of Banville's parody of Hugo.

Izambard later claimed that he had given the young Rimbaud not only Hugo's *Notre-Dame de Paris*, but Banville's play *Le Gringoire*, 'an eminently perverse work'; this latter title inspired Rimbaud's 'Bal des pendus' (Dance of the Hanged Men; *oc*, 80–81), composed a few days after he had to read it for school. In addition – and again, according to Izambard – it led directly to Rimbaud contacting Banville. Just as important, it offers another way to connect the dots between all three poets, as Banville humbly dedicated his play 'À Victor Hugo'. Nineteenth-century French poetry was thus a fabric rich with the interwoven tensions in which the very nature of being a poet meant being wrapped up in a complex intertextual relationship of inspiration, borrowing, rejecting and plagiarizing; and on this score Arthur Rimbaud was no exception.

A few months after his letter to Banville, Rimbaud wrote to Izambard with lavish praise – this time of the sincere variety – for two other poets who had just published new volumes. First was Louisa Siefert and the poem 'Marguerite' from her collection *Rayons perdus* (1869), with a beauty that reminded Rimbaud of Sophocles; the other was a poet called Paul Verlaine. Rimbaud described Verlaine's collection *Fêtes galantes* (1869) as 'extremely strange, very funny; but really, it's adorable. Sometimes with serious licence' (*oc*, 332), and as an example of such licence he quoted the line 'Et la tigresse épouvantable d'Hyrcanie' (And the terrible tigress of Hyrcania), with 'épouvantable' (terrible) thumbing its nose at poetic convention by straddling the alexandrine line's caesura ('Et la tigresse épou[+]vantable d'Hyrcanie') and splicing the word 'épouvantable' in two so that the parts sound like 'époux vantable', or 'laudable spouse'. Of course, there is little subtlety to Verlaine's placing of something terrible, something literally *meaning* 'terrible', centre stage in a verse and in such a way that its very terribleness and its transgression would immediately jump off the page towards most readers of the day. (No amount of prescience would be sufficient to grasp, in late 1870, the extent to which Rimbaud

Étienne Carjat, *Paul Verlaine*, 1870.

would witness at first hand how Verlaine could drive a wedge into a praiseworthy spouse and make the spouse truly *épouvantable*.)

To be sure, such subversions of poetic verse do not a revolution make – Rimbaud's own poetic revolution was still a little over a year away – but, like the poetic licence that he found so endearing in Verlaine's poem, the 'que' in 'Ah! Quel beau matin que ce matin des étrennes' from 'Les Étrennes des orphelins' is an early example of the pressure that Rimbaud's verse would inflict on the walls of French poetry: cracks in the foundation. In a similar way, and despite its gentle pastoral wandering, the heart of 'Sensation' brings more subversive potential than one might think, and Rimbaud's continued resistance to rules remains deeply poetic and deeply *personal*: the dieresis in 'bohémi-en' not only stretches out the wandering by an extra syllable, but it does so through a disordering or undoing of rules at the centre of the lyric, the possessive 'mi-en' (mine) standing in for the first-person subject, the 'je' with whose emotions we readers become so intimately acquainted, the centre of emotion, language, metre and beauty. Despite being the bedrock of poetry since Aristotle, such lyric subjectivity was merely another brick in the wall for Rimbaud, who even in his earliest poems saw through it and how to exploit it, like a cat toying with a mouse under its paw. As this diaeresis underscores the subject's destabilized nature, Rimbaud reclaims a disjointed subjectivity in the midst of this attribute – bohemian – that very specifically assigns identity to the state of not being pinned down to any place, and certainly not being contained within any four walls.

In addition to offering another early glimpse into the dislocation in Rimbaud's verse poetry, 'Sensation' also marks the start of his connection to Parnassian poetry. In the letter to Banville that served as its frame (*oc*, 323–30), Rimbaud's profusion of punctuation and his repeated insistence on his naiveté and his youth are hints that he is yet again openly playing with the letter's addressee: 'Dear *Maître*, We are in the months of love; I am seventeen. The age of hope and dreams, they say – and now I have begun, a child touched by the finger of the Muse – excuse me if this is banal – to express my good beliefs, my hopes, my sensations, all those things dear to poets – and this I call the spring'. What's more, he exaggerates his exuberance with tongue firmly planted in cheek and with a possible suggestion to his private parts: 'it is because I love all poets, all good Parnassians . . . *Anch'io*, gentlemen of the press, I will be a Parnassian! I do not know what is inside me . . . that wants to come out . . .'. Rimbaud piles on a panoply of clichés, knowing full well that Banville will recognize them to be ideas of Romanticism that were rejected by other Parnassians but that Banville still accepted, thereby making this letter to be a sort of missive in code, as if to say, *you and I are the only ones left who still appreciate these tired ideas*. Banville – and Parnassian poetry in general – very much embody the political, legal and literary establishment; and so Rimbaud simultaneously flirts with that mode of acceptability and pokes it in the eye. In the same stroke, into his own treatise of what it takes to be a real poet, he adds his roadmap, his way out of Charleville: 'In two years, in one year perhaps, I will be in Paris.'

The map full of escape routes through the Ardennes remained foremost in Rimbaud's mind; just as important were the growing pressures of the war that France had declared on Prussia on 19 July. Walls were closing in on Rimbaud, and – whether they were made of Ardennais granite or Parnassian rhythms – they were borders to be crossed and limits to be trespassed, always starting points for whatever lay beyond.

2

Fields

When Rimbaud was not sending letters to established poets
hoping to be included among the Parisian literary elite, he was
criss-crossing the countryside around Charleville, making the
kinds of connections between the pastoral and the poetic that he
expressed in 'Sensation'. Blazing paths through the Ardennais
landscape produced a number of poems, including 'Ma Bohême
(Fantaisie)' (My Bohemian Life (Fantasy)); *oc*, 106). It is a poem of
and for a vagabond that trades in images of space, poverty, tactile
sensations and inspiration; a series of itineraries simultaneously
intimate and wide-reaching, physical and ethereal:

> *Je m'en allais, les poings dans mes poches crevées;*
> *Mon paletot aussi devenait idéal;*
> *J'allais sous le ciel, Muse! et j'étais ton féal;*
> *Oh! là là! que d'amours splendides j'ai rêvées!*
>
> *Mon unique culotte avait un large trou.*
> *– Petit-Poucet rêveur, j'égrenais dans ma course*
> *Des rimes. Mon auberge était à la Grande-Ourse.*
> *– Mes étoiles au ciel avaient un doux frou-frou*
>
> *Et je les écoutais, assis au bord des routes,*
> *Ces bons soirs de septembre où je sentais des gouttes*
> *De rosée à mon front, comme un vin de vigueur;*

Où, rimant au milieu des ombres fantastiques,
Comme des lyres, je tirais les élastiques
De mes souliers blessés, un pied près de mon cœur!

I went off, fists in my torn pockets; / My coat too was becoming ideal; / I walked under the sky, Muse! And I was your vassal; / Oh! la la! what brilliant loves I dreamed of! // My only pair of trousers had a big hole. / – Tom Thumb in a daze, as I went along I sowed / Rhymes. My inn was at the Big Dipper. / – My stars in the sky made a soft rustling sound // And I listened to them, seated at the side of the road, / Those good September evenings when I felt drops / Of dew on my brow, like a strong wind; // Where, rhyming in the midst of fantastic shadows, / Like lyres I plucked the elastics / Of my wounded shoes, one foot near to my heart!

The poem's lyrical journeys stretch far and run deep – 'I went off', 'I walked', 'I went along' – as the first-person subject produces a poetic universe all his own, all around him. It is his bohemian experience, after all, and the title's parenthetical appendage blurs the boundaries between fields crossed by poet, lyric subject and reader: the pastoral and all the senses, all of it worn down from constant movement. Furthermore, and inherent in the nineteenth-century use of the word 'fantaisie', there are structural fields that are crossed: between form and freedom, between contingency (innovation and breaking rules) and overdetermination (following rules in spite of it all). 'Ma Bohême' is a good example of the tension between the rule-bound form of the sonnet and fantastical rule-breaking playfulness and its subversions of lyrical seriousness. The lofty 'ideal' is a coat; pockets have holes; the overly exuberant start of line 4 makes a mockery of effusive love; and the subject, played by a dazed Tom Thumb, pulls his foot (with worn-out, tired shoe) close to his heart, the source of lyric poetry.

Easily recognized are both the form of the sonnet itself – which in the French context follows the Petrarchan model imported from Italy in the sixteenth century – and the liberties that Rimbaud brings to it. For starters, he flaunts the rule whereby a 'volta', or turn, traditionally marks the break between a sonnet's two quatrains (four-line stanzas) and the two tercets (three-line stanzas) that follow them. After spilling over the end of line 6 via an enjambment – when one line of poetry straddles, or flows into, the next – that results in the isolation of the leftover words 'Des rimes' at the start of the next line, the poet goes an audacious step further and runs the second stanza into the third, connecting them not only with the conjunction 'Et' at the start of line 9 but with the sound 'ou', emphasized by the silly and onomatopoetic 'doux frou-frou' as well as in the end-line rhymes (to which he had just drawn our attention with the words 'Des rimes') 'trou' / 'frou-frou', 'course' / 'Ourse', and 'routes' / 'gouttes'. But there is more, and we would be excused for wondering if 'des lyres' are here in the plural because they produce the homophonous 'délires', perhaps the best way to explain the poetic delirium that is unfolding. Once again, a rhyme is the key: 'fantastiques' / 'élastiques' point to this poem's elasticity. Straying far from rules of poetic rhythm, this 'fantaisie' offers a number of asymmetrical ways to get through the line with, most notably: 'Comme des lyres, je' + 'tirais les élastiques' (l. 13). The presence of the lyric subject 'je' in the sixth position makes it impossible to find symmetrical order in this verse, since the 'je' forms a grammatical unit with the verb with which it is conjugated ('je tirais') and thus leads the reader towards an unconventional rhythm in which the caesura is attacked and undermined. With this clearly heard and felt discordance, it becomes difficult to read this line other than as a satirical mockery of the lyric. Such insolent treatment of certain basic tenets of traditional French versification is supported by the poem's insistence on feet, which refer both to the source of the wandering steps and to the beats that make up poetic rhythm.

Rimbaud is not only wearing out the soles of his feet; he is running roughshod over the field of French poetry.

If Rimbaud's wanderings and flights led him from Charleville through nature to new experiences and towards poetic innovations (or 'fantaisie') to express it all, the fields that he crossed were soon themselves altered as well. For less than two months after he sent three poems to Banville, France declared war against Prussia, on 19 July: upon the commencement of hostilities, eastern France would quickly be turned from fields of wandering to fields of war. At the same time, Izambard left for the summer holiday in his hometown, the northern city of Douai; with each passing day Rimbaud had fewer and fewer reasons to stay put. A few weeks later he moaned to his teacher:

> You are lucky, *you are!*, to no longer be living in Charleville! – My native town is supremely stupid among all the little provincial towns. You see, on that subject, I no longer have any illusions. Because it is beside Mézières – a city that you can't find on a map [. . .] I am at a loss, ill, mad, stupid, astounded; I had hoped for sunbaths, long walks, rest, travel, adventure, bohemian larks, in a word; especially I had hoped for newspapers and books . . . But there is nothing! Nothing! The mail no longer delivers anything to bookstores; Paris is coyly making fun of us: not a single new book! Everything is dead!' (*oc*, 330–31)

Little wonder, then, that he looked to flee. But rather than 'Any Where Other Than Charleville', he had a specific place in mind; at the end of August, Rimbaud hopped on a train to Paris, without telling anyone and without any money. Upon his arrival at the Gare du Nord he was arrested for not having a train fare and imprisoned in Mazas prison (across from the Gare de Lyon; it has since been destroyed). In addition to the unadvisable practice of travel without proper fare during wartime, it should be said that

Rimbaud's arrival at the train station was itself a bit of an event; according to his childhood friend Ernest Delahaye, Rimbaud was arrested for seditious speech and resisting arrest, for he shouted, 'Down with General Trochu!' as soon as his feet hit the train platform (the career soldier Louis-Jules Trochu had just been named governor of Paris). To that account, Izambard alleged that the police searched Rimbaud and relieved him of papers whose hieroglyph-like scribblings made them wonder if he was a spy or a thief, before putting him in a holding cell and then taking him to Mazas.

Days later, while some French troops were besieged in Metz, others withdrew towards Sedan, where the last major battle of the war ended on 2 September; Prussians overwhelmed the French and took Napoleon III prisoner along with some 100,000 of his soldiers. The Second Empire fell, and on 4 September the Third Republic was declared. Amid this political turmoil, Rimbaud wrote to Izambard, who agreed to send money to have him released from Mazas. Upon his arrival in Douai a few weeks later, Rimbaud stayed for a few weeks at the home of Izambard's in-laws, the Gindre family. Before he left to return to Charleville he entrusted fifteen poems to Izambard's friend, the poet and editor Paul Demeny. Rimbaud no doubt hoped that they would be published, for he brought a meticulous care to his manuscripts: large, clear titles adorned poems written in a very legible penmanship, each one with a forceful (if not exuberant) signature. As Izambard explained, his young student copied the poems carefully on large, fresh sheets of paper; at the slightest error he would start with a fresh page, and as soon as he ran out he asked for money for more. When one of the Gindre sisters suggested that he turn a sheet over and write on the back, he admonished her and explained that sending a double-sided manuscript to a publisher simply wasn't done (*JJL*, 165).

As for their intended reader: Demeny was active in the Parisian poetry scene, as co-founder and co-editor of the Librairie artistique, which published his own collection of poems, *Les Glaneuses* (1870). The back cover of Demeny's volume proudly boasted the other poets in the publisher's list, announced as 'Contemporary poets not published by A. Lemerre'. The 'etc., etc., etc.' that trailed the names suggests a steady, if not robust, string of poetic production within this alternative to the dominant Parnassian wave. None of the authors of the Librairie artistique would find success for their poetry; anyone wishing to pursue postgraduate study today on the poems of Albert de Massougnes, Édouard Snéod (the nom de plume of Édouard Doens) or Albert Sarboris will find no competition (that is, if they can obtain the volumes of poetry in the first place). If Demeny is the only one of these non-Parnassians to be remembered today, it is much less for his forgettable verse than for the role he had in preserving Rimbaud's verse – and the missed opportunity for the Librairie artistique. The publishing house that never published the Charleville native would soon close its doors, leaving Demeny saddled with mountains of debt. For his part, Rimbaud would continue criss-crossing northeastern France: a new fugue in the first week of October to Charleroi in Belgium, where he tried to find work as a journalist; then a return to Douai in mid-October ended with a knock on the door by a gendarme, whom Mme Rimbaud had sent to retrieve him and bring him home. He would leave Demeny seven more poems, no doubt hoping that, if Banville wouldn't help him get published among the Parnassians, then Demeny could publish all 22 poems he had left with him as a volume for the Librairie artistique. Before we judge too harshly this mediocre poet and even less successful publisher, though, we should be thankful for what was undoubtedly his most important failure: not following through on a friend's request. The following year, in June 1871, Rimbaud would write to Demeny with examples of his new poems and ask him to burn all of the old ones that he had been stupid enough to leave with him in Douai; his poetic world view was on the verge of total upheaval. For whatever reason, Demeny was

Paul Demeny, *c.* 1870.

not moved by his friend's request. The poems didn't get close to the fire, and today they are commonly referred to as the *recueil Demeny*.[1]

At the same time, political events continued to draw Rimbaud's attention. When his school took up a collection to support the army fighting Prussia, Rimbaud refused to participate. In the same letter to Izambard in which he said that being in Charleville and Mézières was the equivalent of being nowhere, he expressed his displeasure with what he referred to as 'patrouillotisme' – a word that refers to overly zealous patrolling at the same time that it mocks patriotism – preferring pacifism to the ongoing military campaign: 'My country is rising up! . . . I prefer to see it seated: keep your boots still!, that's my slogan' (*oc*, 330–31). The fall of the Second Empire at Sedan (just a dozen miles from Charleville) and the proclamation of the Third Republic inspired him to write the sonnet 'Rages de Césars' (Caesars' Rages; *oc*, 91). In it, Rimbaud rails against the recently disgraced Napoleon III – himself a poor imitation of his uncle, Napoleon I, whose empire and image the nephew attempted to recreate, desperately, incessantly, pathetically – and voices the optimism of the new republic, exclaiming:

> *Car l'Empereur est soûl de ses vingt ans d'orgie!*
> *Il s'était dit: 'Je vais souffler la Liberté*
> *Bien délicatement, ainsi qu'une bougie!'*
> *La Liberté revit! Il se sent éreinté!* (ll. 5–8)

For the Emperor is drunk on his twenty years' orgy! / He had said to himself: 'I will blow out Liberty / Very softly, like a candle!' / Liberty lives again! He feels his back is broken!

The Siege of Paris, which began on 17 September, only added to Rimbaud's fervour, and he attempted to enlist, alongside Izambard, in the Garde nationale in Douai. Unable to take up arms because he was too young, he accompanied his teacher to the daily training exercises on the city ramparts and picked up his pen instead, writing a letter of protest (signed F. Petit) in which he insisted that the mayor of Douai support the Garde with weapons. He continued writing, and his prose was finally well received by an editor: none other than Izambard himself. During his brief stint as editor of *Le Libéral du Nord* he published, on 25 September, Rimbaud's account of an electoral meeting held in Douai two days earlier. Two months later, Rimbaud's political views would again make the papers, this time in a short-lived Charleville daily called *Le Progrès des Ardennes*. The paper was edited by Émile Jacoby (nom de plume of Philippe-Émile Jacobs), the writer and photographer who had taken the photograph of Arthur and Frédéric Rimbaud on the day of their first communion. Rimbaud and Delahaye both used pseudonyms for the submissions they sent Jacoby, because *Le Progrès des Ardennes* was politically radical compared to its more staid competitor, *Le Courrier des Ardennes*; Delahaye became Dhayle, while Jean Nicolas Arthur Rimbaud retained his first Christian name and flipped the syllables of his surname to become Jean Baudry. Rimbaud's submissions were not immediately successful, for in the issue of Wednesday 9 November the paper published a short paragraph that read:

> – *To Mr J. Baudry, in Charleville.* – Impossible to include your verses at the present time. What we need are articles of current affairs and having an immediate usefulness. Once the enemy will no longer be on our soil, we will perhaps have the time to take up our reed pipes and sing about the arts of peace. But today, we have other things to do. (*oc*, 846–7)

Baudry answered the call, for a little over two weeks later, *Le Progrès des Ardennes* published a prose text entitled 'Le Rêve de Bismarck (Fantaisie)' (Bismarck's Dream: A Fantasy; *oc*, 113–14). In it, Otto von Bismarck dozes off as his mind and hand wander over a map of Europe, as dreams and his index finger inch west towards Paris.

Between dreamlike political fantasies and poetic verses that he sent or gave to editors and poets in Charleville, Douai and Paris, Rimbaud's attempts to make a name for himself as a writer and his perpetual motion throughout northeastern France underscored the tension that the sixteen-year-old carried with him in late 1870. Part and parcel with the youthful optimism of his early poems came restlessness: traces of friction. They formed well-trod paths across grassy fields of Ardennais and northern farmland and they appeared as the holes in his trouser pockets in the first lines of 'Au Cabaret-Vert, cinq heures du soir' (*oc*, 111), written after Rimbaud traipsed some 80 kilometres (50 mi.) north of Charleville to Charleroi, in the direction of Brussels. To the poem's warm, pastoral scene Rimbaud adds some tinges of other elements of his Ardennais

Ernest Delahaye, aged 22, *c.* 1875.

upbringing: pulling into a rural bar for a bite to eat, the sustenance all around him more than compensates for his crumbling boots and whatever weariness he must have felt after being on his feet for a week straight, as the opening line suggests ('Depuis huit jours, j'avais déchiré mes bottines'; For a week my boots had been torn apart). As was the case in 'Ma Bohême', the worn-out feet are perceptible in the verse itself. Not only is the poem replete with enjambments, but the irregular caesura in 'Depuis huit jours, j'avais [+] déchiré mes bottines' splits the verb in two and thus tears through poetic language just as the subject's boots place additional tearing at his feet. Two lines later there is an isolated lyric 'je', followed by a number of caesurae that disrupt traditional order and symmetry and cut through grammatically indivisible phrases or highlight particular attributes: '*Au Cabaret-Vert*: je [+] demandai des tartines' (*At the Cabaret-Vert*: I asked for bread; l. 3); 'Quand la fille aux tétons + énormes, aux yeux vifs' (When the girl with the huge tits and lively eyes; l. 8; 'énormes' modifies 'tétons'); 'Du jambon tiède, dans [+] un plat colorié' (Warm ham, in a coloured plate; l. 11); 'D'ail, – et m'emplit la chope [+] immense, avec sa mousse' (Of garlic, – and filled my enormous mug, with its foam; l. 13; 'immense' modifies 'chope').

While such poetic liberties are important signs of a larger poetic revolution to come, they are not unique to Rimbaud. The prodigious student and voracious reader was already fully aware of Hugo's popularization of what is now commonly called the *alexandrin trimètre* or *alexandrin romantique* (trimeter alexandrine or romantic), which divides the meaning and syntax of an alexandrine line into three parts, 4–4–4. Hugo had famously boasted 'J'ai disloqué / ce grand niais / d'alexandrin' (I dislocated that great fool, the alexandrine) in a poem from his collection *Les Contemplations*. Similarly, Rimbaud had already expressed his admiration for Verlaine's poetic licence in *Fêtes galantes*; such modulations within and departures from traditional structures of French versification opened the door for similar liberties in Rimbaud's poems, such as 'Au Cabaret-Vert'.

In this poem, even if the lyric subject doesn't get what he asks for – he asks for half-cooled ham and when the waitress brings it, it is still warm – he nevertheless benefits from many of the inn's other comforts. He can easily surpass the simple images on the walls with a few strokes of his quill, as Rimbaud is doing before our eyes with his irreverent poetics. There is also the laughter, the fun, the levity and the sexual overtones – neither raunchy nor entirely innocent – as we look through the subject's eyes at the lovely, laughing specimen whom he appreciates and who is no doubt whiter, rosier and more flavourful than the ham. In the late afternoon sun, the prize is more than the glistening foam, and his beer mug is not the only thing overflowing, for the poem itself is doing just that: verses flowing into the next in a series of enjambments that create an almost unstoppable rhythm, verses bursting at the seams as are the subject's titillated senses.

When they weren't setting the stage for a celebration of arousal, the Ardennais fields were marked by the war that cut through them. The intrusion of war into the countryside was an obvious inspiration for 'Le Dormeur du val' (The Sleeper in the Valley; OC, 112), one of the poems that Rimbaud might very well have sent to *Le Progrès des Ardennes* for consideration (the claim that *Le Progrès* published it in November 1870 has not been verified, as no copies of the publication have been found).

Few poems are better known; for its beauty and varying degrees of simplicity and complexity, generations of French schoolchildren have had to memorize it. Its rhyme scheme of *rimes croisées* (ABAB CDCD) in the first two stanzas does not follow the traditional sonnet pattern of a *rime embrassée* (ABBA ABBA) in the quatrains:

C'est un trou de verdure où chante une rivière
Accrochant follement aux herbes des haillons
D'argent; où le soleil, de la montagne fière,
Luit: c'est un petit val qui mousse de rayons.

Un soldat jeune, bouche ouverte, tête nue,
Et la nuque baignant dans le frais cresson bleu,
Dort; il est étendu dans l'herbe, sous la nue,
Pâle dans son lit vert où la lumière pleut.

It is a green hollow where a river sings / Madly catching on the grasses / Silver rags; where the sun atop the proud mountain /

Shines: it is a small valley which bubbles over with rays. //
A young soldier, his mouth open, his head bare, / And the
nape of his neck bathing in the cool blue watercress, / Sleeps;
he is stretched out on the grass, under clouds, / Pale on his
green bed where the light rains down.

Nevertheless, the 'volta' offers a clear shift in such formal details,
as the tercets' EEF GGF rhymes do follow one of the two traditional
variants to sonnet rhymes:

Les pieds dans les glaïeuls, il dort. Souriant comme
Sourirait un enfant malade, il fait un somme:
Nature, berce-le chaudement: il a froid.

Les parfums ne font pas frissonner sa narine;
Il dort dans le soleil, la main sur sa poitrine
Tranquille. Il a deux trous rouges au côté droit.

His feet in the gladiolas, he sleeps. Smiling as / A sick child
would smile, he is taking a nap: / Nature, cradle him warmly:
he is cold. // Odours to not make his nostrils quiver; / He sleeps
in the sun, his hand on his breast, / Silent. He has two red holes
in his right side.

It is not the rhyme scheme that makes this poem so famous, but
rather its last line, the *chute*, or fall: the sudden surprise at the
end that sheds new light on the poem's meaning and leads to a
reconsideration of all that came before. For the reader who arrives
for the first time at the end of 'Le Dormeur du val', the final verse
rarely fails to pack a punch; it sends shock waves back through
the rest of the poem and gives new meaning to the calm, tranquil
immobility that seemed as idyllic as the pastoral scene in which
the 'sleeping' soldier lay. The two red holes – reinforced by the

insistence on the number two and the assonance in 'deux tr*ou*s
r*ou*ges' (an echo of the earlier 'b*ou*che *ou*verte') – are not the only
signs of the intrusion of the Franco-Prussian War into the bucolic,
though; nature's seemingly reassuring warmth and tenderness
masks the foreshadowing of danger evident not only in the open
mouth but in the pale complexion, the gladiolas and the sick
child. Other elements portend trouble: namely, the disruption
of the alexandrines through the numerous enjambments and
the buckshot of punctuation that rips through the poem. These
phenomena are combined twice in the first stanza (lines 2–4)
and once in the second (lines 6–7), and the practice continues in
the tercets as punctuation pumps more holes into the poem (lines
9–11, 13–14). The sweet silence of the bucolic offers a similarly
sober indictment of war, not by fighting fire with poetic fire but
by evoking, through the lyric, all that the war threatens, and ruins:
the right to live in peace, in harmony with nature, with all of the
senses activated. The poem's sources of bliss – an uncovered head
basking in the sun's warmth, the coolness of watercress, the grass
underneath an outstretched body, the pleasant scents that the nose
can discover – are all mirages: war deprives us of such pleasures.
Rimbaud's presentation of the horrors of war is brilliant precisely
for the fact that the violence comes not from the graphic nature
with which the fallen soldier is described but in the last line's
instantaneous jolt and its dismantling of the warm and tender
natural scene. On the one hand, one would be hard-pressed to find
a less gory corpse, in this poem about a body shot and left for dead;
on the other, the body of poetry is pierced with shots throughout
these fourteen verses, and the field of language is littered with
detritus. In just two short shots ('deux trous rouges'), war upends
the entire tableau and ruins it all, leaving readers with mouth agape
just like the soldier himself.

The last vestiges of Ardennes' pastoral charm destroyed
and littered with carnage, Rimbaud had yet another reason to

find the region lacking, and so he looked further afield for new opportunities. Paris remained foremost in his sights not merely for the poetic opportunities he imagined there but for the different fields of vision that the metropolis offered. It was the epitome of the modern city, as Baudelaire – whom Rimbaud would describe as 'the first seer, king of poets, *a real god*' – had presented it so well in the 'Tableaux parisiens' section of *Les Fleurs du mal* and as he would do again in his prose poems collected under the title *Le Spleen de Paris*. Rimbaud had a modern, urban backdrop in mind when he set Greek mythology on its ear in 'Vénus Anadyomène' (*oc*, 65):

> *Comme d'un cercueil vert en fer blanc, une tête*
> *De femme à cheveux bruns fortement pommadés*
> *D'une vieille baignoire émerge, lente et bête*
> *Avec des déficits assez mal ravaudés;*
>
> *Puis le col gras et gris, les larges omoplates*
> *Qui saillent; le dos court qui rentre et qui ressort;*
> *Puis les rondeurs des reins semblent prendre l'essor;*
> *La graisse sous la peau paraît en feuilles plates:*
>
> *L'échine est un peu rouge, et le tout sent un goût*
> *Horrible étrangement; on remarque surtout*
> *Des singularités qu'il faut voir à la loupe . . .*
>
> *Les reins portent deux mots gravés: Clara Venus;*
> *– Et tout ce corps remue et tend sa large croupe*
> *Belle hideusement d'un ulcère à l'anus.*

As from a green zinc coffin, a head / Of a woman with brown hair heavily pomaded / Emerges slowly and stupidly from an old bathtub, / With bald patches rather badly hidden; // Then

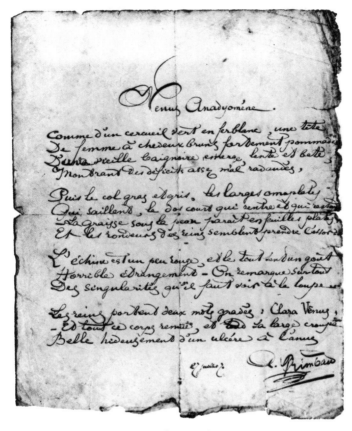

Arthur Rimbaud, 'Vénus Anadyomène', manuscript.

the fat grey neck, broad shoulder blades / Sticking out; the short
back which curves in and bulges; / Then the roundness of the
buttocks seems to take off; / The fat under the skin appears in
slabs: // The spine is a bit red; and the whole thing has a smell
/ Strangely horrible; you notice especially / Odd details you'd
have to see with a magnifying glass . . . // The buttocks bear two
engraved words: *Clara Venus*; / – And that whole body moves

and extends its broad rump / Hideously beautiful with an ulcer on the anus.

The birth of Venus is most often depicted as rising from the waters, as suggested by the source for her Greek name (Aphrodite comes from *aphros*, foam) and for the titular word *anadyomene*, she who emerges. If the most famous depiction is Botticelli's *The Birth of Venus* (1486), which today hangs in Florence's Uffizi Gallery, during Rimbaud's childhood Alexandre Cabanel had famously exhibited his own version of the same in the 1863 Salon. An immediate hit, Cabanel's painting was purchased by Napoleon III for 20,000 francs and put on the walls of the Élysée Palace in 1865. Of the many writers who reported on Cabanel's painting at that Salon, none other than Émile Zola had a passing thought along the same lines as Rimbaud:

> Take an ancient Venus, any woman's body drawn according to sacred rules, and, lightly, with a tuft, make this body up with blush and rice powder; you will have Monsieur Cabanel's . . . At the Champ de Mars, go look at *la Naissance de Vénus*. The goddess, drowned in a river of milk, looks like a delicious lorette; not in the flesh – that would be indecent – but in a kind of white and pink almond paste.[2]

If it would be indecent to say that the goddess looks like a lorette – a synonym for courtesan, the name taken from the Notre-Dame-de-Lorette neighbourhood in Paris where many such women lived in the mid-nineteenth century – then what would it be to turn Venus into a tattooed woman, which at the time was well-known code for saying that she was a prostitute? What would it mean to add insult to that already injurious poetic depiction by taking the goddess's graceful birth, traditionally rising out of the foamy waters, and replacing it with the clumsy lurching from out of a filthy bathtub, the only kind of movement that her unhealthy, malodorous rolls of fat will allow her? How much further can indecency be pushed by the final rhyme – for again, Rimbaud exploits the sonnet's *chute* and saves the best for last – of '*Venus*' and 'anus'? As if taking a page from Baudelaire's *Les Fleurs du mal* (The Flowers of Evil), in which there is beauty to be found, for example, in the maggots oozing out of the rotting corpse of 'Une charogne' (A Carcass), Rimbaud gives the goddess of beauty an ulcer. What's more, he won't let us look away, and instead forces our attention to details that require the use of a magnifying glass. This poem responds particularly well to the etymological origin of the word 'ulcer', coming from the Latin *ulcus*: a sore or, figuratively, a painful subject.

It is a painful subject to read about and to envision, and the poem inflicts pain on the Parnassian aesthetic as well: not least since Rimbaud's poem also draws on Albert Glatigny's poem 'Les Antres malsains', the final poem of his collection *Les Vignes folles* (1860; the collection was dedicated to Banville). Thus when Rimbaud declared to Banville that he was a true Parnassian, he was, while genuinely wishing to be published, also more than a bit lacking in sincere adherence to any aesthetic approach. Instead of the Parnassian preference for forms carved into marble that both preserves their beauty and immobilizes them (thus leaving them completely defenceless against the source of the male poetic gaze), Rimbaud sets his beauty in motion, as awkward as that motion may be. Instead of the impassive, detached observation that the Parnassians brought to their poetic world view, we roll up our sleeves to discover 'The fat under the skin [that] appears in slabs' and we come out of this scene with dirt under our fingernails and the odour still lingering in our nostrils. Similarly awkward and troublesome to the Parnassian preference for order is this poem's departure from traditional sonnet rhyme scheme, for Rimbaud uses *rime croisée* (ABAB) in the first stanza and *rime embrassée* with a new rhyme (CDDC) in the second one.

Enjambments wreak additional havoc on traditional poetic rhythm: in the first line, a comma after the ninth syllable creates a secondary break in the line that severs the woman's head, 'une tête'. Other combinations of punctuation and enjambments create additional moments of textual emphasis in 'les larges omoplates / Qui saillent [. . .] (ll. 5–6), 'le tout sent un goût / Horrible étrangement' (ll. 9–10), and 'Les reins portent deux mots gravés: *Clara Venus*' (ll. 12). This last line is particularly pointed as its caesura splits 'deux mots' from 'gravés': words from how they are written. If the 'mien' / 'bohémien' rhyme in 'Sensation' amounted to a wink when Rimbaud sent it to Banville, then the heightened awareness of the act of writing to which 'Vénus Anadyomène' bears witness makes this poem a dirty poke in the Parnassians' eyes. Rimbaud's poetry was moving at a breathtaking pace: a mere five months after trying to ingratiate himself to the literary establishment, the young poet was pushing beyond his contemporaries by breaking them down and making fun of them. Putting behind him what he perceived as their intellectual and structural rigidity, he could only look to a future full of new fields of expression, open and inventive.

With such anti-Parnassian verve and with a growing displeasure for Charleville, where he found himself after the gendarme's escort brought him back to the protective embrace of 'la Mother', Rimbaud kept looking ahead. Immediately upon his return he wrote to Izambard and while envisioning a 'liberté libre' (free freedom), he simultaneously promised to stay put and heed his teacher's advice (and perhaps stop showing up on his Douai doorstep, since Rimbaud was quickly wearing out his welcome). At the same time that he promised to earn Izambard's friendship by not giving in to the temptation to flee again, he showed how very hard it was to resist, and if he could do so today, tomorrow would be another day:

Arthur Rimbaud, letter to Georges Izambard, 2 November 1870.

Monsieur,

– This is for you alone. –

I returned to Charleville the day after leaving you. My mother took me in, and here I am . . . with nothing to do. My mother will not put me back in school before January '71.

So you see? I kept my promise.

I am dying, I am decomposing in dullness, in paltry wickedness, in grayness. What can I say? – in a terrible way I insist on worshipping free freedom, and so many things that one would say 'that's pitiful', isn't it true? I was to set out again today. I could have done so. I had new clothes on, I would have sold my watch, and long live freedom! – But I stayed back! I stayed back! – I will want to leave many more times – Let's go, hat, coat, my two fists in my pockets and we're off! But I will stay, I will stay. I didn't promise to. But I will do so to deserve your affection: you told me as such. I will deserve it.

The gratitude I feel for you, I could not express today any more than any other day. I will prove it to you. If it were a question of doing something for you, I'd die in order to do it, – I give you my word. – I still have so many things to say . . .

– This 'heartless'

A. Rimbaud[3]

Despite his sincere promise to keep his word, he couldn't, and wouldn't. He simply had to leave his family and Charleville. The fields of the Ardennes were not enough; Paris's Elysian fields kept calling, and he had to find a way to get back there – preferably with a train ticket.

3

Capital

As Rimbaud was dealing with his restlessness and his desire to leave staid Charleville, the rest of France was in upheaval, reeling from the loss of the Franco-Prussian War and the fall of the Second Empire. After the victory in Sedan, Prussian armies had marched with little opposition to Paris, where their siege began on 17 September 1870. To say that Parisians were miserable during the Prussian occupation would be an understatement of massive proportions; with no heat through the cold winter months and rapidly deteriorating conditions more generally, they saw a spike in disease. With little access to food and precious few alternatives, they resorted to eating everything they could. Horses, dogs, cats and rats went first. When that supply ran out, they turned to the animals in the Jardin des Plantes zoo; restaurant menus of late 1870 offered such exotic dishes as *cuissot de loup, sauce chevreuil* (wolf haunch in a deer sauce), *terrine d'antilope aux truffes* (terrine of antelope with truffles), *civet de kangourou* (kangaroo stew) and *chameau rôti à l'anglaise* (camel roasted à l'anglaise). The zoo's two elephants, Castor and Pollux, also made their way into a restaurant kitchen. Pigeons were spared, for they – like hot-air balloons – were among the only means of mail service, and thus communication, in and out of the city. In late January 1871, French Vice President Jules Favre's capitulation to the Prussian chancellor Otto von Bismarck in Versailles created a provisional armistice that allowed the starving Parisians to eat again. The French government paid a terrible price, in all respects:

200 million francs, a Prussian victory parade down the Champs-Élysées in Paris, and occupying troops stationed along the city's eastern border until the indemnity was paid and armistice was complete.

The Parisians would have none of it. Disgusted by the failure of their own government, incensed by the terms of the armistice and by the sight of German troops marching victoriously through their city, the increasingly radicalized Garde nationale wanted to keep fighting. When armed forces loyal to the French government went to recover cannons from Montmartre on 18 March, the Garde nationale surprised the soldiers and chased them away. Chief executive of the Third Republic Adolphe Thiers called the army back to Versailles to regroup and plan its next move. In the resulting vacuum the Parisians elected a socialist city government and referred to its insurrection as *la Commune*. It put forth a broad radical agenda that had wide support from the left-leaning working-class inhabitants (many members of the middle and upper classes had fled the city during the siege). This power-sharing government established a series of commissions to run the city – indeed, similar communes were planned throughout France – ruling without president, mayor or commander-in-chief. Under the red socialist flag, the Commune pushed for new workers' rights, abolished the death penalty and military conscription, and reinstated the French Republican calendar (a rejection of its Gregorian counterpart's royalist and religious influences). In the name of the separation of Church and state, Church property was declared public property and religious practice was banned from schools. Decades before feminism would begin to take hold in France, proposals were made for gender and wage equality, a woman's right to divorce, and professional education for girls. On 10 May the Treaty of Frankfurt brought an official end to the war, with France accepting to pay 5 billion francs and losing much of Alsace and Lorraine; in 'Le Rêve de Bismarck' Rimbaud had written 'Triomphant, Bismarck a couvert de son index l'Alsace et la Lorraine!' (Triumphant, Bismarck covered Alsace and Lorraine with his index finger). But the Commune waged on; it lasted for a total of 72 days. On 21 May the French army stormed back into Paris, setting off the *semaine sanglante* (bloody week), a massacre that ended on 28 May after somewhere between 6,000 and 10,000 deaths. As the army worked its way through the Communards' barricades, the retreating forces set fire to a number of buildings throughout the city, including the Hôtel de Ville (City Hall), where a certain Paul Verlaine had recently been working as an office clerk. The week's most infamous moment was when hundreds of Communards were lined up along the wall of the Père-Lachaise cemetery's southeast corner, shot, and thrown into a common grave. To this day, every year on 1 May groups pay homage to the fallen insurgents in front of what is known as the *Mur des Fédérés* (Communards' Wall).

For Rimbaud, the year 1871 began in a manner similar to how 1870 ended: with a trip to Paris. Let it not be said that the brilliant student ignored his lessons; his time in Mazas must have been fresh enough in his mind, since he obtained proper train fare – by hawking a watch – for his next flight from Charleville, in late February 1871. During his two weeks in Paris and despite the turmoil and harrowing living conditions, literature remained his primary focus, and he spent his time window-shopping at the addresses he no doubt knew by heart: at Alphonse Lemerre's bookshop in the passage Choiseul and at Demeny's Librairie artistique at 18 rue Bonaparte. Not particularly interested in the literary establishment – for he could have met the Parnassians in their late-day gatherings in Lemerre's shop – he took stock of new publications and plays that were being performed. Much of it focused on war; as he wrote to Demeny, 'It seems that every paper has its *Siège*, its *Journal du Siège*' – and as Émile Jacoby had written to 'Jean Baudry' the previous year, aesthetic pursuits were still not the word of the day.

When he went to the Librairie artistique, Rimbaud knew that the editor would not be in – Demeny was in Abbeville, on military duty, with Izambard – and he used his connection to the editor to try to obtain the address of the journalist and soon-to-be Communard Eugène Vermersch and, perhaps through Vermersch, that of the caricaturist André Gill. Gill and Vermersch had begun collaborating in 1866 in the pages of *Le Hanneton: journal des toqués*, which Vermersch had founded a few years prior. From Rimbaud's interest in Gill's caricatures – which became a mainstay, famously adorning covers of the journal *La Lune* – and in the biting satire and virulent anti-imperial fervour of writers such as Vermersch and Jules Vallès, it seems clear that Rimbaud was already looking beyond the Parnassians and their politically detached *l'art pour l'art* approach.

Either from Vermersch or from someone at the Librairie artistique who trusted this sixteen-year-old who claimed that he knew Demeny, Rimbaud obtained Gill's address, at 89 rue d'Enfer (today avenue Denfert-Rochereau). When he arrived, the key was in the lock – apparently such was Gill's common practice – and Rimbaud let himself in. From there, stories vary; according to one version, Rimbaud instantly made himself at home by sleeping on the divan until Gill returned, discovered this child he didn't know, woke up this uninvited guest who was snoring loudly and asked him to explain himself. In a different telling, it was Rimbaud who woke Gill up, expressing his admiration for Gill's work and presenting himself as a great poet. Either way, the combination of a unique set of circumstances for a first encounter and Gill's legendary generosity – having fallen on hard times himself, he was always quick to lend an aspiring artist or poet a sympathetic ear, if not a place to stay – provide some insight into how some in Paris would find the young poet irresistibly charming despite themselves.

But they wouldn't do so right away. Rimbaud's first prisonless stay in the capital soon ended, and he left, allegedly on foot; in

March he arrived in Charleville after yet another unsuccessful attempt to establish himself somewhere else. On 12 April he took up a job working for *Le Progrès des Ardennes*, sifting through the correspondence that the paper received. After ceasing operations at the end of 1870 because of the Prussian invasion, Jacoby had revived the daily newspaper in March. That Rimbaud's job lasted only for five days is really not his fault: the government shut down the *Progrès* on the 17th for being sympathetic to the Commune.

In Charleville in March, Rimbaud just missed his brush with history, since the Commune was about to begin in Paris. Then again, he was about to launch a revolution of his own. Refusing to return to the Collège de Charleville when it reopened in mid-April, he had his mind on what the future would hold both in Paris and in poetry, as he explained in the two letters that have come to mean so much – for Rimbaud's poetry as well as for modern literature.

These two letters from mid-May 1871 are commonly called the *Lettres du Voyant* (Seer Letters). In the first, written to Izambard on 13 May (*OC*, 339–41), Rimbaud squarely situates his poetic labours in the events of the day, and he contrasts his new poetic project with his former teacher's dutiful work and lifeless poetry, becoming only slightly disrespectful in the process. Two days later, he writes a longer version to Demeny (*OC*, 342–9), presenting 'an hour of new literature' and a treatise on nothing less than the past, present and future of French poetry. The first of the letters is addressed to Monsieur 'Isambart'; it is unlikely that Rimbaud could have misspelled his favourite teacher's name by accident, and so it is possible that Izambard started to get the message before he even opened the envelope.

Even though he knew his student to be precocious, the teacher was doubtless stunned when he started reading the letter, for Rimbaud ridicules everything his elder stands for and offers a revolution to take its place. Unlike Izambard, who is dutifully contributing to society by toiling in the rut of teaching and composing horribly insipid 'poésie subjective', Rimbaud declares that he is on strike, and that his new brand of 'poésie objective' will fill the void of work, duty and convention. As he explains:

> Why? I want to be a poet, and I am working to make myself a *Seer*: you will not understand this, and I don't know how to explain it to you. It is a question of reaching the unknown by the derangement of *all the senses*. The sufferings are enormous, but one has to be strong, one has to be born a poet, and I know that I am a poet. This is not all my fault. It is wrong to say: I think. One ought to say: people think me. – Pardon the pun.[1]
>
> I is someone else. Too bad for the wood which finds itself a violin and Scorn for the heedless who argue over what they are completely missing!
>
> You are not a *Teacher* for me. I give you this: is it satire, as you would say? Is it poetry? It is fantasy, always. – But I beg you, do not underline it with your pencil or too much with your thought:
>
>   'Le Cœur supplicié' [The Tortured Heart]
>   My sad heart slobbers at the poop
> [. . .]
> This does not mean nothing. – <u>*Answer me*</u>: chez Mr Deverrière, for A.R.
>
>   Warm greetings,
>
>   Ar. Rimbaud

It is also just as likely that this letter's two grammatical peculiarities jumped off the page for the teacher who read them: first, the jarringly incorrect verb conjugation of 'Je est un autre' (I is someone else) in the penultimate paragraph and, after the poem, the double negative in the assertion 'Ça ne veut pas rien dire' (This does not mean nothing). The former is Rimbaud's now famous formulation for his 'poésie objective' superior to Izambard's (and the Parnassians', and the Romantics') 'poésie subjective'; neither a cold, objective perspective nor an attention solely on objects, the new approach is far less dependent on the subject that had dominated lyric poetry from its very beginnings. An entirely new perspective is in order; instead of the source of poetic creativity, the 'Voyant' is the filter through which objects are expressed. It is more than a minor reference to the lyre – the traditional source of poetry – that the project of 'voyance' draws on musical instruments: wood and brass find themselves transformed into a violin and trumpet, respectively. Like these raw materials, Rimbaud discovers that he, too, has become a medium for artistic expression. Furthermore, the poet becomes 'Voyant', as the second letter announces, through 'le dérèglement de *tous les sens*' (the derangement of *all the senses*). The phrase refers in no small part to Baudelaire – whom Rimbaud calls 'the first seer, king of poets, *a real god*' in his letter to Demeny – and to Baudelaire's notion of synaesthesia, the juxtaposition of senses that are usually experienced separately. Rimbaud calls upon the senses by means of their 'dérèglement', the undoing of their rules ('règles'): their disorganization or de-regimenting amplifies and surpasses any previous connections they might have had. In addition, the phrase from the letter to Demeny insists on the 'long, immense et raisonné dérèglement de *tous les sens*'; this vast poetic project is very much a reasoned and deliberate dismantling and deconstruction, rather than a random disordering for chaos's sake. Finally, the 'Voyant' sees objects and form as they appear: as Rimbaud explains to Demeny while comparing the poet to Prometheus, 'if what he brings back from *down there* has form, he gives form; if it is formless, he gives formlessness.' The ramifications for poetic form are clear: instead of being limited to applying preconceived notions and conventions, the 'Voyant' lets the form (or lack thereof) emerge, and he merely renders the poem as it imposes itself on him.

When he was done insulting Izambard, Rimbaud included the poem 'Le Cœur supplicié' (*oc*, 340) and insisted on its importance by drawing his former teacher's attention to the blatantly obvious double negative. The poem would reappear, slightly modified, several more times: in a letter to Demeny the following month as 'Le Cœur du pitre' (The Clown's Heart), and among poems recopied by Verlaine from late 1871 under the title 'Le Cœur volé' (The Stolen Heart). Precisely what it 'doesn't not mean' – or, rather, what part of its meaning Rimbaud wished to signal to Izambard – is less clear. The first of its three eight-line stanzas portrays the pitiful scene of the subject who is ridiculed by soldiers, leaning over the stern of a ship and about to be sick:

Mon triste cœur bave à la poupe . . .
Mon cœur est plein de caporal!
Ils y lancent des jets de soupe,
Mon triste cœur bave à la poupe . . .
Sous les quolibets de la troupe
Qui lance un rire général,
Mon triste cœur bave à la poupe,
Mon cœur est plein de caporal!

My sad heart slobbers at the poop . . . / My heart covered with tobacco-spit! / They spew streams of soup at it, / My sad heart drools at the poop . . . / Under the jeering of the soldiers / Who break out laughing, / My sad heart drools at the poop, / My heart covered with tobacco-spit!

The 'triste cœur' that dominates here gives way to the soldiers themselves as their actions turn from jeering laughter to physical violence in the second stanza. Sadness and pity are immediately replaced by sorrow as the soldiers brutally sodomize the subject, replacing jeering with rape:

Ithyphalliques et pioupiesques
Leurs insultes l'ont dépravé;
À la vesprée, ils font des fresques
Ithyphalliques et pioupiesques;
Ô flots abracadabrantesques,
Prenez mon cœur, qu'il soit sauvé!
Ithyphalliques et pioupiesques,
Leurs insultes l'ont dépravé!

Ithyphallic and soldierish, / Their insults have depraved it; /
At vespers, they make frescoes / Ithyphallic and soldierish;
/ O abracadabratic waves, / Take my heart, let it be saved! /
Ithyphallic and soldierish, / Their insults have depraved it!

Rimbaud was perhaps intimating to his former teacher that the
poem didn't not refer to some similar treatment he had endured
while incarcerated in Mazas; it requires even less of an interpretive
stretch to read into this poem's preponderance of military terms
and violent attack of the subject's heart the similarly violent
repression and rape of the Commune in Paris – France's heart –
by soldiers of the French army. Above all, this poem illustrates
Rimbaud's new approach to 'poésie objective': an anti-lyricism,
with a multilayered approach to words (polysemy would soon
become one of his calling cards) and increased symbolic presence.
More compelling than any possible autobiographic reality is the
poem's evocation of distress and pathos and the final stanza's
question of what to do next:

Quand ils auront tari leurs chiques,
Comment agir, ô cœur volé?
Ce seront des refrains bachiques
Quand ils auront tari leurs chiques!
J'aurai des sursauts stomachiques

Si mon cœur triste est ravalé!
Quand ils auront tari leurs chiques,
Comment agir, ô cœur volé?

When they have used up their quid, / What to do now, O stolen
heart? / There will be Bacchic refrains / When they have used
up their quid! / I will have stomach retchings / If my sad heart
is degraded! / When they have used up their quid, / What to do
now, O stolen heart?

Finally, there is the unmistakable nature of Rimbaud's provocation
by including it in this letter in the first place, for the pointed
question 'Comment agir, ô coeur volé?' marks an abrupt shift from
the parodic weight of his earlier criticism of Izambard.

Two days later, Rimbaud sent other examples of his new poetics
to Demeny, announcing, 'I have decided to give you an hour of
new literature. I begin at once with a song of today.' The first poem,
'Chant de guerre parisien' (Parisian War Song; *oc*, 342–3), parodies
a poem by François Coppée at the same time as it imagines the
ongoing battle in Paris as a burlesque song that calls Republican
leaders Adolphe Thiers and Ernest Picard out by name and pits the
Communard and Versaillais forces against each other. The war song
begins with an irreverent tone, declaring that what is obvious in this
war song is not war but springtime:

Le Printemps est évident, car
Du cœur des Propriétés vertes,
Le vol de Thiers et de Picard
Tient ses splendeurs grandes ouvertes!

Spring is evident, for / From the heart of green Estates, / The
theft/flight[2] of Thiers and Picard / Holds wide open
its splendours!

This stanza also offers an example of what Rimbaud had noticed during his visit to Paris a few weeks earlier, for Alfred Le Petit had written some similar verses in the caption to a caricature of Picard that bore the title 'Souvenir du Siège de Paris', recalling Rimbaud's comment that 'It seems that every paper has its *Siège*, its *Journal du Siège*'. It is certainly possible that Rimbaud's 'car' / 'Picard' rhyme – alongside of which he wrote 'What rhymes! Oh! What rhymes!' in the letter to Demeny – is inspired by Le Petit's verses 'Paris a beaucoup souffert, car / Il a souffert qu'Ernest Picard' (Paris has greatly suffered, for / It puts up with Ernest Picard).

After the war song that he declares is 'Neither joke, nor paradox', Rimbaud launches into a discussion of 2,000 years of poetry: inherited from the Greeks, it has been mouldy since Racine. His explanation of the tenets of his newly developed approach ends at that holy grail of poetry, the unknown:

All forms of love, suffering and madness. He searches himself. He exhausts all poisons in himself and keeps only their quintessences. Unspeakable torture where he needs all his faith, all his super-human strength, where he becomes among all men the great patient, the great criminal, the damned one – and the supreme Scholar! – Because he reaches the *unknown*! Since he cultivated his soul, rich already, more than any man! He reaches the unknown, and when, bewildered, he ends by losing the intelligence of his visions, he has seen them! Let him die as he leaps through unheard of and unnameable things: other horrible workers will come; they will begin from the horizons where the other one collapsed!

– To be continued in six minutes –

Here I insert a second psalm *to accompany the text*: please lend a friendly ear – and everyone will be delighted. – I have the bow in hand and I begin:

'Mes petites amoureuses' [My Little Lovers]

[. . .]

Drawing the bow across the strings – little matter if it was in this letter that he used his brass/trumpet metaphor, and the wood/violin was in the earlier letter to Izambard – he sadistically enumerates the steps in his amorous deception with his next poem's ugly little lovers, putting them through their paces in a grotesque dance that isolates their body parts one by one. Somehow Rimbaud is able to spin an ironic web of eroticism, cruelty, aggression and love, as misogyny courses through the ballerinas' syncopated movements. He then closes his letter with even more irony, sending Demeny a final poem: 'And let's close with a pious hymn.' The poem is hardly pious: entitled 'Accroupissements' (Squattings), it details Brother Milotus's three daily defecations.

As he had done to Izambard, Rimbaud implores Demeny to respond: 'You would be loathsome not to answer: quickly, because in a week, I will be in Paris, perhaps.' But he wouldn't be. One week later he was still in Charleville, and he was there the following week while the Versaillais troops were gunning down Communards in front of the *Mur des Fédérés*. Unquestionably inspired by the political events unfolding at breakneck pace and the radically new ways of thinking about urban space that they created,[3] he was not there to witness them in person. Instead, transformations in the political and the social became increasingly apparent in Rimbaud's poetic space, as he proceeded to dismantle verse poetry with greater urgency. Such was the context in which he sent Demeny the letter in June asking him to burn the poems left in Douai; in their place, he proposed a clear break from his earlier poetry with three new poems inspired by the Commune and its social imperatives of class, poverty and violence: 'Les Poètes de sept ans' (Seven-year-old Poets), 'Les Pauvres à l'église' (The Poor in

Church) and 'Le Cœur du pitre' (The Clown's Heart). Other poems from this period similarly reflect a political and social awareness: 'L'Orgie parisienne ou Paris se repeuple' (Parisian Orgy or Paris is Repopulated) and 'Les Sœurs de charité' (Sisters of Charity). Rimbaud's political engagement was apparently not limited to the poetic; Delahaye claimed that in August he read a communist constitution that Rimbaud had drafted, heavily inspired by the Commune's principles.

And so the political and poetic battles raged on; in August Rimbaud wrote again to Banville and sent him a new, 160-line poem entitled 'Ce qu'on dit au Poète à propos de fleurs' (What is Said to the Poet Concerning Flowers; *oc*, 148–54). Just above his own initials Rimbaud had signed the poem 'Alcide Bava' (Heracles Drooled). Banville/Bava: the drooling signature mocks Banville and implicates him in the poem. Less clear is whether 'À Monsieur Théodore de Banville' is meant to be the start of the letter's address or a prefatory element to draw Banville in further – or both – as the recipient will soon be fused with the poet in the poem.

À Monsieur Théodore de Banville

———

Ce qu'on dit au Poète
à propos de fleurs

Ainsi, toujours, vers l'azur noir
[. . .]

Monsieur et Cher Maître,
Vous rappelez-vous . . .

[Thus, always, towards the black azure, / Monsieur and dear Maître [Master], / Do you remember . . .]

Where can we possibly situate poetic voice – and, more to the point, where can Banville situate poetic voice – in a poem in which the poet-recipient is mentioned before the allegorized Poet in the title, long before he is spelled out in line 29, 'Quand BANVILLE en ferait neiger' (When BANVILLE made some snow come down), all of this in a poem that was sent to Banville himself? What kind of relationship is Rimbaud constructing here between poetry, voice and identity? All of these questions and we haven't even begun to read the poem.

The very first verse is a calque of the first line from Lamartine's 'Le Lac'; the famous opening line, 'Ainsi, toujours poussés vers de nouveaux rivages' (Thus always pushed towards new shores), becomes, in Rimbaud's poem:

> *Ainsi, toujours, vers l'azur noir*
> *Où tremble la mer des topazes,*
> *Fonctionneront dans ton soir*
> *Les Lys, ces clystères d'extases!* (ll. 1–4)

Thus, always, towards the black azure, / Where shimmers the sea of topazes, / The Lilies, clysters of ecstasy, / Will function in your evening!

Rimbaud replaces new shores – symbols of new discoveries, each one a comforting suggestion that the poetic voyage will always arrive safely on some new territory – with 'azur', turning the blue (and, figuratively, the heavens) a menacing black: into the great beyond, with no safe landing spots. That the allegorized Lilies are described as enemas of ecstasy marks a clear departure from the traditional relationship between man and nature, amid the other familiar trappings of the lyric: trembling, the topaz of the sea, the evening. The future dominates, as 'Fonctionneront', pronounced with dieresis ('fon-cti-on-ne-ront'), gobbles up five of the line's eight syllables. The departure from earlier poetry is further distilled by the rapidity of the first line, as Rimbaud boils down Lamartine's alexandrine and cuts to the heart of the matter: without the superfluous 'poussés' – that is, the lyric motivation that is part and parcel of the 'poésie subjective' that Rimbaud has left for dead – he can get there more quickly. Similarly, the reduction from 'vers de nouveaux rivages' to 'vers l'azur noir' – four syllables instead of six – replaces the coherence provided by the alliteration of the letter 'v' ('*vers* de nou*v*eaux ri*v*ages') with the more menacing soundscape via the repetition of 'r' in 'vers l'azur noir'. There is more impending doom for the lyric, and thus an open threat to Banville, through the exaggerated repetition of lilies and the roses and more exotic flora later in the poem, underlined by the repetition of 'toujours' (in the first line and recurring in lines 16, 17, 37 and 41), insisting on poetry's tired representation of nature: always the same thing.

It is in the final two sections of the poem that 'Alcide Bava' adapts poetry to meet the values of bourgeois society: Poet is conflated with Merchant, verses become commodities like sodium or rubber, and the juxtaposition of progress and technology produces absurd, outlandish images in support of this manifesto of utilitarian poetry:

Commerçant! colon! médium!
Ta Rime sourdra, rose ou blanche,
Comme un rayon de sodium,
Comme un caoutchouc qui s'épanche!

De tes noirs Poèmes, – Jongleur!
Blancs, verts, et rouges dioptriques,
Que s'évadent d'étranges fleurs
Et des papillons électriques!

Voilà! c'est le Siècle d'enfer!
Et les poteaux télégraphiques

Vont orner, – lyre aux chants de fer,
Tes omoplates magnifiques!

Surtout, rime une version
Sur le mal des pommes de terre!
– Et, pour la composition
De Poèmes pleins de mystère

Qu'on doive lire de Tréguier
À Paramaribo, rachète
Des Tomes de Monsieur Figuier,
– Illustrés! – chez Monsieur Hachette! (ll. 141–60)

Alcide Bava
A. R.

14 juillet 1871

Merchant! colonial! medium! / Your Rhyme will well up, pink or white, / Like a blaze of sodium, / Like a bleeding rubber-tree! // But from your dark Poems, – Juggler! / White, green, and red dioptrics, / Let strange flowers burst forth / And electric butterflies! // There now! it is the Century of hell! / And the telegraph poles / Will embellish, – lyre with iron voice, / Your magnificent shoulder blades! // Above all, put in rhyme a tale / On the potato blight! / – And, for the composition / Of Poems full of mystery // That are to be read from Tréguier / To Paramaribo, buy / Some Volumes of Monsieur Figuier, / – Illustrated! – at Monsieur Hachette's!

This scene is, obviously, ridiculous, and once again Rimbaud is sending Banville a letter with verses that cannot be taken too seriously. And yet: it is all dead serious, and the only question is whether Banville gets it. This last point is driven home even further by what Rimbaud writes after the letter. For starters, what better way to subtly announce a revolution than to backdate it to *le 14 juillet*, date of the French Revolution, and to set it in his own revolutionary year of 1871? This time, he does not ask Banville to publish his poem: he reminds the *maître* of the poems he had sent him earlier and asks, 'Ai-je progressé?'. Given the playfulness in these letters to Banville, the question might be less the literal 'Have I made any progress?' and more along the lines of *are you able to notice my progress?* or, perhaps, the more pointed *have I progressed beyond you?*

A few weeks after leaving his bomb of drool on Banville's doorstep, Verlaine's friend Auguste Bretagne recommended that Rimbaud write to Verlaine. Rimbaud did just that, and he sent Verlaine five poems: 'Les Effarés' (The Frightened Ones), 'Accroupissements' (Squattings), 'Les Douaniers' (The Customs Men), 'Le Cœur volé' (The Stolen Heart) and 'Les Assis' (The Seated Men). As he had copied Sully Prudhomme and Hugo, so would Rimbaud continue to borrow, this time from Verlaine, about whom he had told Demeny in May, 'the new school, called Parnassian, has two seers: Albert Mérat and Paul Verlaine, a real poet.' As his letters to Banville show how cleverly he could use a poem to convey a particular message, Rimbaud's decision to send Verlaine 'Les Effarés' was similarly astute, for it demonstrated the young poet's ability to flatter. Verlaine could not have missed seeing that Rimbaud had lifted a pair of rhymes directly from the opening lines of his own poem 'En bateau' (On a Boat) from *Fêtes galantes*:

L'étoile du berger tremblote
Dans l'eau plus noire, et le pilote
Cherche un briquet dans sa culotte.

The shepherd's star trembles / In the darker water and the pilot / Looks for a lighter in his trousers.

The unmistakable echoes in Rimbaud's missive arrive at the end of the 'Les Effarés': flipped, with altered spelling, and offered as if a conclusive note:

> *Si fort, qu'ils crèvent leur culotte*
> *Et que leur lange blanc tremblotte*
>   *Au vent d'hiver.*

So hard, that they burst their trousers / And their white linen flutters / In the winter wind.

Both the letter that included these poems and Verlaine's response are lost, but Delahaye reported what is now Verlaine's famous reply from September 1871 (along with money for train fare): 'Venez, chère grande âme, on vous appelle, on vous attend' (Come, great dear soul, we call you, we are waiting for you). Delahaye said that before leaving, Rimbaud read him 'Le Bateau ivre' (The Drunken Boat), the poem that Rimbaud had written with the intention of wowing the Paris literary elite. About 'Le Bateau ivre' much has been said, including the famous story – again, told by Delahaye – about when Rimbaud finally found himself face to face with Banville: in late 1871, when Verlaine presented the young poet to *le maître* at the latter's apartment. After Rimbaud read him the poem, Banville said that he should have begun with something more direct, like 'I am a boat who . . .'. Upon leaving his host, Rimbaud made clear to Verlaine how little he thought of Banville: 'C'est un vieux con' (*JJL*, 347). This unverifiable anecdote aside, what is certain is that there would be no turning back, no longer any thought about connecting with the old. Rimbaud's poetry would irrevocably look forward, in leaps and bounds.

'Le Bateau ivre' is an important allegorical transposition of the poetic project laid out in the *Lettres du Voyant*. Its first five stanzas describe the drunken boat breaking its anchors and shaking loose from them: such is the poet breaking with the norms of poetry, with conventions of morality and with the dominant ideology of Western society. Its middle section evokes the wreck's maritime adventures; tossed to and fro by a combination of the sea and the boat's own drunkenness, the poet arrives at the great unknown. The last eight stanzas detail the lyric subject's exhaustion and nostalgia for the old world: the moment when, panicked, the 'Voyant' resigns himself to a form of death, abandoning his visions with nothing other than the consolation of having seen them. This poem's relatively simple and realistic tableau offers an illustration of 'le dérèglement de *tous les sens*': reflections of the sun on the surface of the waters, atmospheric accidents, sunset, and night and dawn on the ocean. But this series of seascapes is broken apart just as quickly as it is produced, and the boat's drunkenness produces a dizzying effect – referred to in the poem as a 'ballet' – with its sudden changes of decor and rhythmic interruptions from displaced caesurae and enjambments, all of which create a frenetic and sputtering pace that parallels the voyage of the poet-as-boat. And yet, the pull of the poetic voyage of self-discovery is too great, as in the famous line 'O que ma quille éclate! O que j'aille à la mer!' (O let my keel burst! O let me go into the sea!; l. 92); the repetition and symmetry in the two so well-balanced halves give equal weight to the two parallel desires for poetic adventure and for writing. Realism then turns towards the fantastic as the sea symbolizes the unknown through the image of the shipwreck and the richness of the poetic language on display: rhythms, musicality, colours, unexpected word associations, rare words or neologisms, effects of synaesthesia and unusual metaphors.

If such a new poetic vocabulary and desire to plunge the depths of the unknown was sure to impress the literary establishment, it would be a particularly bad fit for Verlaine's in-laws, the bourgeois Mauté de Fleurville family. Paul and his young wife Mathilde were living under the same roof as her parents in the family house at

14 rue Nicolet. Mathilde had been instantly smitten with the up-and-coming poet ten years her senior when she met him through her half-brother, the musician Charles de Sivry. Verlaine had already published his first poems in *Le Parnasse contemporain* in April 1866; his first collection, *Poèmes saturniens*, would come out with Lemerre in November of that same year. He and Mathilde met in June 1869, soon after the publication of his second volume, *Fêtes galantes* (Lemerre, 1869). Their courtship inspired his next collection: *La Bonne Chanson* (Lemerre, 1870) was published just before they were married. When Rimbaud arrived from Charleville in late September 1871, Mathilde must have been shocked to see how young he was: she was born in April 1853, making her a year and a half older than Rimbaud. Since she was just seventeen, and eight months' pregnant with the couple's son, Georges (born 30 October 1871), she was in no condition to endure the havoc that Rimbaud and Verlaine would soon wreak on the Mauté de Fleurville household. Clearly, they would have to spend most of their time elsewhere.

And so they did, by attending the dinners of the Vilains Bonshommes, a primarily Parnassian group who since 1869 had been gathering to eat, drink, sing songs and write poetry. At their meetings chez Gustave Pradelle in the rue Cassette, the regulars included Verlaine, Jean Richepin, Maurice Bouchor, Jean Aicard, Ernest d'Hervilly, Émile Blémont, the Cros brothers (Antoine, a doctor; Charles, the poet and inventor who had invented the paleophone eight months before Edison patented the phonograph; and sometimes their sculptor and glass artist brother Henry), André Gill, Léon Valade and Maurice Rollinat. Rimbaud's arrival in the capital coincided with the return to their activities, which had been interrupted by the war. Soon after Verlaine invited him to Paris, he brought the young poet to the group's dinner on 30 September 1871. A week later, Valade described the evening to Blémont, who had missed it:

Invitation to the monthly dinner of the Vilains Bonshommes.

Paul Verlaine, a self-portrait with his friends Valade and Mérat, at a Vilains Bonshommes dinner, Café du Théâtre Bobino.

You missed out by not attending the latest dinner of the horrible Bonshommes . . . There was unveiled – under the auspices of his inventor Verlaine, and his John-the-Baptist-of-the-Left-Bank (yours truly) – a *frightful* poet not yet eighteen, called Arthur Rimbaud. Big hands, big feet, an absolutely *childish* face like that of a thirteen-year-old, with deep blue eyes and a personality more wild than timid: such is this kid whose imagination, full of unheard of powers and perversions, fascinated or terrified all of our friends: 'What a beautiful subject for a preacher,' cried [Jules] Soury. D'Hervilly said: 'Jesus in the midst of the doctors'. [Edmond] Maître told me: 'It is the devil!', which led me to this improved formula: 'The Devil in the midst of the doctors!' I can't give you the biography of our young poet other than to say that he comes from Charleville, and has firm plans of never again seeing his home or his family. – Come see his poetry, and you'll judge for yourself. Unless Destiny is playing one of its tricks on us, this is a *genius* we have before us. (*IJL*, 344)

As Valade's enthusiasm suggests, Rimbaud's reading of 'Le Bateau ivre' was well received. Stéphane Mallarmé penned a similarly warm description about the moment when his and Rimbaud's paths crossed, saying his younger confrère possessed

The *éclat* of a meteor, ignited with no other motive than its own presence, coming out of nowhere and burning out. Certainly all would have existed since, without this considerable passer-by, as no literary circumstance had really prepared it; but the personal case persists, with force. . . .

I didn't meet him, but I saw him, once, at one of the literary meals, thrown together hastily at the end of the War – the dinner of the Vilains Bonshommes . . .[4]

Despite this auspicious start, it would soon go downhill from there. The Commune had driven a wedge through the group, with the more left-leaning members following Charles Cros and splintering off in October to form the more radical (and anti-Parnassian) Cercle Zutique: saying 'zut' (damn) to the establishment, wherever they could find it. (The more conservative elements remained with the Vilains Bonshommes until it disbanded, towards the end of 1872.) The Zutistes met upstairs in the Hôtel des Étrangers, on the corner that looks out on the boulevard Saint-Michel from between the rue de l'École-de-Médecine and the rue Racine. Ernest Cabaner tended bar, played the piano and taught the young poet some basic notions of the chromatic scale. One day Rimbaud crossed the river and went to 10 rue Notre-Dame-de-Lorette: specifically to the photography studio of fellow Zutiste Étienne Carjat. Since Verlaine had sat for photographs there the previous year, it is probable that he was present when Carjat took the famous portrait of Rimbaud that is among the most iconic images in all of French literature.

As Rimbaud was hoping to catch on with the Zutistes, he was quickly burning bridges. He was certainly not welcome at the home of the Mauté de Fleurville family. (Mathilde said that the first time she ever saw lice was on the filthy poet's pillow after he left the household. When she mentioned it, her husband laughed and said that he liked to keep them in his hair so he could flick them at priests he might see.) After leaving the rue Nicolet, Rimbaud stayed at the Hôtel des Étrangers in exchange for working as Cabaner's assistant; when that arrangement soured Charles Cros took him in. Once he left the apartment at 13 rue Séguier that Cros shared with the painter Michel Eudes (called Michel de L'Hay, also called Pénoutet), Rimbaud bounced around the Latin Quarter, quickly wearing out his welcome everywhere he went. After staying with Cros, Gill and Cabaner he even spent a few days chez Banville, in a mansard that the 'vieux con' provided

Étienne Carjat, portrait of Arthur Rimbaud, *c.* 1871.

above his own apartment at 10 rue de Buci. The list of grievances – apocryphal at best – grew with each move: while chez Cros he tore his host's poems out of journals and used them as toilet paper, and upon discovering that the housekeeper had cleaned and waxed his boots, he quickly ran to the street to soil them again, bringing the filth back inside; Félicien Champsaur's *roman-à-clef Dinah Samuel* (1882) alleges that Rimbaud stole from Gill; finally, while in Banville's attic he stood naked in front of the windows throwing shreds of clothes up and over the roof, he broke the wash-pot and a mirror, and he sold whatever furniture was still intact. The poet who had written 'On n'est pas sérieux, quand on a dix-sept-ans' (We aren't serious when we're seventeen) twice in his 32-line poem 'Roman' (Novel, *oc*, 88–9) was proving the point convincingly. His behaviour was growing more and more unpalatable, even to those who were inclined to be sympathetic; after a group of writers went to the opening night of a play by Albert Glatigny, Verlaine's childhood friend Edmond Lepelletier published the following account (under the pseudonym Gaston Valentin) in *Le Peuple souverain* the next day, 16 November 1871:

All of Parnassus was there, people and conversation filling the foyer, under the watchful eye of its editor Alphonse Lemerre. Here and there one could see the blonde Catulle Mendès arm in arm with even blonder [Albert] Mérat. Léon Valade, [Léon] Dierx and Henri Houssaye chatted as well. The Saturnian poet Paul Verlaine had on his arm a charming young person, Mademoiselle Rimbaut [*sic*]. All in all, an excellent night for the Odéon theatre.

Despite all the drama, the Cercle Zutique continued to meet regularly and produce well-lubricated scribblings called the *Album zutique*, a collection that would be passed around for some ninety years before finally being published as a volume in 1961.[5] These texts and illustrations amount to a series of inside jokes, of varying quality. One important feature is something already evident at the bottom of 'Ce qu'on dit au Poète à propos de fleurs', something the Zutistes took on as a regular practice: in their poems, many of which are parodies, the poem is followed by the false signature of the parodied poet, that signature followed by the initials of the poet who actually wrote the poem. By far the most famous poem to follow this practice is 'Sonnet du Trou du Cul' (Sonnet of/from an Arsehole; *oc*, 171), Verlaine and Rimbaud's parody of Mérat's volume *L'Idole* (The Idol) and its sonnets devoted to different parts of the female body. When Verlaine later reprinted the poem in his homoerotic collection *Hombres* (1904) and in a letter he wrote to Charles Morice in December 1883, he attributed the quatrains to himself and the tercets to Rimbaud:

L'Idole.
Sonnet du Trou du Cul.

Obscur et froncé comme un œillet violet
Il respire, humblement tapi parmi la mousse
Humide encor d'amour qui suit la fuite douce
Des Fesses blanches jusqu'au coeur de son ourlet.

Des filaments pareils à des larmes de lait
Ont pleuré, sous le vent cruel qui les repousse,
À travers de petits caillots de marne rousse
Pour s'aller perdre où la pente les appelait.

Mon Rêve s'aboucha souvent à sa ventouse;
Mon âme, du coït matériel jalouse,
En fit son larmier fauve et son nid de sanglots.

C'est l'olive pâmée, et la flûte câline;
C'est le tube où descend la céleste praline:
Chanaan féminin dans les moiteurs enclos!

> Albert Mérat.
> P. V. – A. R.

Dark and wrinkled like a deep pink carnation / It breathes,
humbly nestled among the moss / Still wet with love that follows
the gentle flight / Of the white Buttocks to the heart of its border.
// Filaments like tears of milk / Have wept, under the cruel
wind pushing them back, / Over small clots of reddish marl /
And there lose themselves where the slope called them. // In
my Dream my mouth was often placed on its opening; / My soul,
jealous of the physical coitus, / Made of it its fawny tear-bottle
and its nest of sobs. // It is the fainting olive, and the cajoling
flute; / It is the tube where the heavenly praline descends: /
A feminine Canaan enclosed in moisture!

This sonnet with well-crafted alexandrines and regular rhyme scheme
is rather self-explanatory, but a look under the hood shows that it is
truly remarkable. It begins with a parody of Mérat, a fellow Zutiste;
written in collaboration, it breaks with the tradition of the lyric as the
source of great personal inspiration; and it celebrates sodomy in
terms openly crude, recognizable to all, and laced with homosexual
argot ('œillet', line 1, means carnation; in slang, anus). What better
way to mock any last vestiges of verse poetry's lofty aspirations than
by sticking the sonnet where the sun don't shine? The profusion of
the letter 'o' in the first line – 'O*bscur et fr*o*ncé c*o*mme un œillet vi*o*let'*
– is a series of reminders of the object at the poem's centre.

Rimbaud's time in Paris was not just for playing around and
scandalizing the Parisian elite, though, for it was also when Rimbaud
wrote 'Voyelles' (Vowels; *oc*, 167), another of his masterpieces.
Some of the inspiration is said to have come from the chromatic

scale taught to him by Cabaner, who coloured the notes and gave each one the sound of a vowel; whatever the source, Rimbaud manufactured a blueprint for poetic creation, again in a sonnet:

A noir, E blanc, I rouge, U vert, O bleu: voyelles,
Je dirai quelque jour vos naissances latentes:
A, noir corset velu des mouches éclatantes
Qui bombinent autour des puanteurs cruelles,

Golfes d'ombre; E, candeurs des vapeurs et des tentes,
Lances des glaciers fiers, rois blancs, frissons d'ombelles;
I, pourpres, sang craché, rire des lèvres belles
Dans la colère ou les ivresses pénitentes;

U, cycles, vibrements divins des mers virides,
Paix des pâtis semés d'animaux, paix des rides
Que l'alchimie imprime aux grands fronts studieux;

O, Suprême Clairon plein des strideurs étranges,
Silences traversés des Mondes et des Anges:
– Ô l'Oméga, rayon violet de Ses Yeux!

A black, E white, I red, U green, O blue: vowels, / One day I will tell your latent birth: / A, black hairy corset of shining flies / Which buzz around cruel stench, // Gulfs of darkness; E, whiteness of vapours and tents, / Lances of proud glaciers, white kings, quivering of flowers; / I, purples, spit blood, laughter of beautiful lips / In anger or penitent drunkenness; // U, cycles, divine vibrations of green seas, / Peace of pastures scattered with animals, peace of the wrinkles / Which alchemy prints on heavy studious brows; // O, Suprême Clarion full of strange stridor, / Silences crossed by Worlds and Angels: / – O, the Omega, violet beam from His Eyes!

Rather than a fundamental part of the 'dérèglement de *tous les sens*', the interplay between vowels and colours is a platform for invention and for the discovery of new associations. The examples trade in approximations, variations on themes, and evocations of similar qualities: red is for blood and lips, green for pastures and seas. Sometimes the relationship is physical: waves follow the shape of the letter 'u' as the bell of a trumpet is visualized in 'O, Suprême Clairon'. But those connections operate on the level of sounds, colours and shapes; meaning is absent, sounds are arbitrary. On the other hand, there is an undeniable logic as the letters follow the conventional sequence of A-E-I-O-U – or, rather, they offer a nod to it, *almost* follow it, and then don't. Rimbaud recognizes conventional order, reproduces it while altering it, and produces a new series that is instantly recognizable as a new take on the old. Upending traditional logic while leaving behind enough of its constituent parts so we can trace his steps makes for a compelling example of 'le dérèglement de *tous les sens*'.

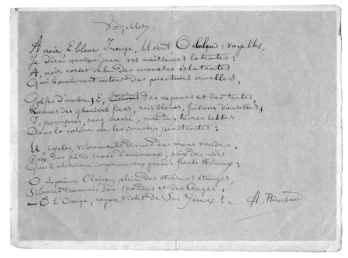

Arthur Rimbaud, 'Voyelles', manuscript.

In fact this search for invention is expressed elsewhere in the letter to Demeny:

> These poets will exist! When the endless servitude of woman is broken, when she lives for and by herself, man – heretofore abominable – having given her her release, she too will be a poet! Woman will find some of the unknown! Will her world of ideas differ from ours? – She will find strange, unfathomable, repulsive, delicious things; we will take them, we will understand them.

Rimbaud is not proposing a proto-feminist manifesto. Nor is he completely insincere, simply spouting off to get a rise out of his interlocutor, throwing things against a wall to see what sticks. Instead, he envisions examples across the broadest spectrum of possibilities for poetic creation, in which women can be creators, poets and sources of the unknown. Indeed, Rimbaud greatly appreciated poets such as Marceline Desbordes-Valmore and Louisa Siefert; but here this brief comment about women becoming poets – 'she too will be a poet', in the future tense – is just one of the many possible manifestations of future creativity and inventiveness that will be shaken free once the rotting tree of 'poésie subjective' is taken down, making way for new life.

Whatever idealized poetic creativity Rimbaud had imagined for the future, he was finding it harder to manage in the present. On 13 January 1872, a drunken Verlaine erupted in rage (apparently his coffee was served cold) and threw his two-and-a-half-month-old son Georges against the wall, before fleeing to his mother's house in the rue Lécluse. He returned the next morning sober and full of remorse, then went back out to spend the day drinking. That night, despite his earlier promises of good behaviour, he forcibly opened Mathilde's locked bedroom door and had to be kicked out by her father; the following day a doctor's examination

Henri Fantin-Latour, *Un Coin de table* (A Corner of the Table), Paris, 1872. Seated (left to right): Paul Verlaine, Arthur Rimbaud, Léon Valade, Ernest d'Hervilly, Camille Pelletan and a vase of flowers (in place of Albert Mérat). Standing (left to right): Pierre Elzéar, Émile Blémont and Jean Aicard.

revealed that her neck showed bruises consistent with attempted strangulation. She fled with Georges, while Verlaine spent increasing amounts of time with Rimbaud, drunk on absinthe in Parisian cafés. Unable to house his young friend at the Mautés' residence, Verlaine rented a room for him in the rue Campagne-Premier. From January to March Rimbaud shared the room with the artist Jean-Louis Forain, whom the poets affectionately called Gavroche: like the character in *Les Misérables*, Forain had served in the war (against Prussia).

By February, Verlaine possessed enough of Rimbaud's poems (most of them recopied in Verlaine's hand) to begin constituting a proper collection. What is today referred to as the *recueil Verlaine* is composed of poems on a series of pages numbered 1 to 24, to which the elder poet added a table of contents. Given the amount of time the poets were spending together during this period, it is hard to imagine that Verlaine would have conceived of a grouping, or even their order, without Rimbaud's input.[6] The following month they attended the Cercle zutique's meeting on 2 March. While Auguste Creissels was reading aloud his poem 'Sonnet de combat', Rimbaud punctuated the performance by shouting 'merde!' at the end of each line. The evening quickly deteriorated: after Carjat called Rimbaud a toad, Rimbaud stabbed the photographer with a sword-cane, either right there or later, waiting for him in the hallway after having been expelled and pouncing on him as he was leaving. Rimbaud was banned from subsequent dinners, Carjat threw away the negative and his copies of the photograph that he had taken of Rimbaud in 1871, and Albert Mérat refused to sit for the group portrait *Le Coin de table* which Henri Fantin-Latour had been painting since January. The work, which would be exhibited in the Salon in May of that year, now hangs in the Musée d'Orsay, and a vase of flowers covers up where Fantin-Latour had traced his initial sketches for Mérat.

The Zutistes had had enough, as had Paris. With nowhere else to turn, Rimbaud could do little more than retreat to Charleville. His stay in Charleville would be brief, though, and he would soon set off again.

Félix Régamey, Rimbaud dozing in a chair, 1872.

4

Cities

No longer welcome in Paris, Rimbaud spent his time in Charleville
visiting various bars with Delahaye. Meanwhile, back in the capital,
Verlaine promised Mathilde that he and Rimbaud were through, and
he convinced her to return to Paris, which she did in mid-March.
Marital order was restored, at least on the surface; behind her back
(and no doubt right under her nose) the two poets maintained a
regular correspondence. When Rimbaud quietly returned to Paris
in early May, the two picked up where they had left off. If Mathilde
might have suspected that something was off when her husband
began returning home drunk with increasing frequency, she
definitely should have begun to worry when he came home bleeding
profusely. That was on 9 May: according to eyewitness Charles Cros,
Rimbaud was playing with a knife while they were drinking in the
Rat Mort café (in place Pigalle) when he suddenly thrust it into
Verlaine's hands and legs. The knife theme would continue in June,
when Verlaine, drunk, threatened Mathilde with one in a restaurant
(the night before, he had attempted to set her hair on fire). That
same month, Rimbaud described his favourite pastime in a letter
to Delahaye, written from 'Parshit' and dated 'June-ish': he exclaims,
'Long live the Academy of Absomphe, in spite of the waiters' ill
tempers' and describes his rhythm of writing through the night
hours, as regular as his absinthe benders during the day (*oc*, 368).

Despite the unorthodox hours that he kept, Rimbaud's intense
period of writing produced a number of poems, commonly referred

to as the *Derniers vers* for being among the last poems he would write in verse: 'Larme', 'La Rivière de cassis', 'Comédie de la soif ', 'Bonne pensée du matin', 'Patience' (initially entitled 'Bannières de mai'), 'Chanson de la plus haute tour', 'Éternité', 'Âge d'or', 'Jeune ménage', 'Est-elle almée? . . .', 'Plates-bandes d'amarantes . . .', 'Fêtes de la faim', 'Ô saisons, ô châteaux . . .', 'Mémoire', 'Entends comme brame . . .', 'Honte', 'Michel et Christine', 'Qu'est-ce pour nous, mon cœur . . .' and 'Les Corbeaux'.

The disrespect that was already evident in Zutiste parodies such as the sonnet in honour of Mérat's volume *L'Idole* grew larger, this time for verse. Unlike the drunken rage that saw him stab Verlaine, here it is with the precision of a surgeon that he sets upon cutting up the alexandrine. Such is the case, for example, in the sixteen-line poem 'Larme' (Tear; *oc*, 207), in which the subject's ineffective potential for representing anything – 'j'eusse été mauvaise enseigne d'auberge' (I would have been a bad inn sign) – runs parallel to his conflation of liquids such as tears, liquor and river water, all of which complicate the poem's emotional frame. Meaning and rhyme are upended with a series of approximations and deliberate near misses: Rimbaud simultaneously recognizes and flouts the rules. Repeated sounds course through the poem's four quatrains, filled with assonances of 'wa' and 'o' in words like 'loin' (far) and 'eau' (water) and combined in 'oiseaux' (birds), creating a sonorous rhythm that detaches the importance of sounds from its traditional location at the end of the line or just before the caesura. This last option is further complicated by the fact that there is no regular caesura: the lines have eleven syllables and thus cannot be split into two halves. Another poem from this period in which verse is torn asunder is 'Mémoire' (Memory; *oc*, 234–5), which bears the last vestiges of the alexandrine, so battered that they are barely recognizable. It is a poem of the obliteration of verse; amid the detritus, a kind of commemoration of what verse used to be. Rules of versification are similarly put on display at

the moment of their obliteration in 'Bonne pensée du matin'
(Good Thought in the Morning; oc, 202), in which the idyll
of a morning-after is not as perfect as it might seem. For what
begins with quatrains of three eight-syllable lines followed by
a six-syllable line – and even announced with a clear temporal
marker, 'À quatre heures du matin, l'été' (At four in the morning,
in summer) – quickly devolves into a lack of order and rhythm, and
an awkward, erratic stumbling through verses that run roughshod
over the very movement of the poem. Lines that would normally
be read as ten syllables have to be pronounced with hasty shortcuts,
elisions between words and other unconventional liberties. The
precise time announced at the poem's outset is a false start, for
the remaining lines offer a near incessant metrical fluctuation
between eight, nine and ten syllables without any discernible
pattern. Rimbaud goes right to the heart of what it means to read
a poem and what internal rules should govern our experience with
it. He then adds insult to injury by literally upending the stanza
at the end of the poem: the fifth and final stanza begins with the
shorter verse first, before the longer ones. Then, as if to make fun
of the poem itself, and perhaps its readers, Rimbaud suddenly
instils the kind of order that would have made the most conservative
versifiers happy, with the alexandrine 'En attendant le bain [+] dans
la mer à midi' (As they wait for the bath in the sea, at noon). This
perfect harmony and symmetry is dripping with irony for – as
Rimbaud knows, on so many levels – you can't go home again:
poetry has moved on from the confines of verse, and each attempt
at bringing it back will only make it more anachronistic.

Verlaine was seeing married life in Paris as increasingly of the
past. He and Rimbaud slipped out of town and made their way to
Brussels, a city that had long been a safe harbour from the Second
Empire censors and conservatism that held sway in Paris. It was
to Brussels that the editor Auguste Poulet-Malassis had fled his
creditors in 1862; from there, he published a number of collections

of poetry, including licentious verses by Baudelaire. In 1867 he produced a collection of five erotic sonnets entitled *Les Amies* written by Verlaine, who was called 'the dismissed Pablo de Herlagnez' on the title page. Just as the two poets had kept a secret correspondence after Verlaine had reconciled with Mathilde, this time Verlaine wrote to Mathilde without Rimbaud's knowledge. Later, in her memoirs, she would quote a letter from memory – 'My poor Mathilde, don't be sad, don't cry; I'm having a bad dream, I'll come back someday'[1] – and claim that Verlaine had asked for her to bring his personal affairs, since when he and Rimbaud slipped out of town he had taken little more than his cane and his hat. Seizing the opportunity, Mathilde went with Verlaine's mother to Brussels in an attempt to get him to leave Rimbaud once and for all. Her pleas seemed to work; Verlaine boarded a Paris-bound train with the two women. Or, rather, they worked for a short while: Rimbaud had secretly boarded the same train, and while it was stopped for customs before crossing over the border into France he convinced Verlaine to change his mind. The two poets were off towards Brussels again, leaving Mathilde to return to Paris, where in early October she would formally request a legal separation, claiming 'disreputable relations' between her husband and Rimbaud.[2]

It was upon the events of these months that a certain Officer Lombard, having been tasked with keeping an eye on the poets, would base his report. Despite some inaccuracies, the story of 'Robert Verlaine' and 'Raimbaud' (with a cameo by 'Charles de Civry') is great melodrama:

The scene takes place in Brussels.
The Parnassian Robert Verlaine had been married for three or four months to the sister of Civry, a composer and pianist who had been imprisoned in Satory after the Commune, shipped off, then released.

The marriage had taken place towards the start or the middle of last year.

The couple was getting on well despite the foolish whims of Verlaine, whose brain went off track a long time ago, when misfortune brought to Paris a young boy, Raimbaud, from Charleville, who came by himself to present his works to the Parnassians. In terms of his morals and his talent, this Raimbaud, aged 15 to 16, was and is a monstrosity.

He has the mechanics of verse like no one; it's just that his works are absolutely unintelligible and repulsive. Verlaine fell in love with Raimbaud, who shared his passion, and they went to Belgium to savour their heartfelt peace and all that follows it.

Verlaine had left his wife with an unmatched light-heartedness, and yet she is reputedly very likeable and well mannered.

The two lovers were seen in Brussels, displaying their affections publicly. A short while ago, Madame Verlaine went there to find her husband, to try to bring him back. Verlaine responded that it was too late, that reconciliation was impossible and that, besides, they could no longer control themselves. 'Married life is odious to me,' he exclaimed. 'We make love like tigers!' and, saying this, he showed her his chest: tattooed and bruised with knife wounds that had been inflicted by his friend Raimbaud. These two beings beat and tore at each other like ferocious beasts, all for the pleasure of making up.[3]

In the meantime, Verlaine and Rimbaud made a go of it: first Brussels to Ostend, then on 7 September they crossed the Channel, arrived at Charing Cross Station and spent their time in what was known as the French Quarter (today Soho). Verlaine described the crossing, which brought them to Dover – 'a mediocre town, with wonderful cliffs' – where they were served eggs and tea: 'This was my first introduction to the English Sunday, which is not so terrible after all.'[4] At one point Verlaine went to Belgium to attempt reconciliation with his wife, but failed and returned to Rimbaud in London, where they become acquainted with many of the former Communards who had remained in London after fleeing Paris. They even moved into the room previously occupied by one of them: Eugène Vermersch, who was moving out as he was about to be married. Their room was at 34–35 Howland Street, in Fitzrovia; just before the building was torn down in 1938, the plaque indicating the poets' presence was donated to Verlaine's hometown of Metz. Their time with the illustrator and former Vilains Bonhommes member Félix Régamey – specifically, in Régamey's studio at 16 Langham Street – inspired verses similar in tone to the Zutiste poems from the previous year, this time based on Régamey's album. The inspiration was reciprocal; Rimbaud scribbled down the poem 'L'enfant qui ramassa les balles . . .'[5] (The Child who Picked up Balls) and Régamey sketched the pair walking in London.

Increasingly worried about Mathilde's legal case, Verlaine and Rimbaud asked Mme Rimbaud to intervene. She accepted, although her attempts in Paris were in vain; she was nevertheless able (with Verlaine's assistance) to convince her son to return to Charleville, where he stayed for a few weeks. Without Rimbaud, Verlaine did not fare well in London, where he was alone with his regrets for having destroyed his marriage and chances at conventional respectability. Depressed and sick, Verlaine sent out various calls for help; Verlaine's mother and Rimbaud responded, the former arriving in time for New Year's and the latter on 3 January 1873. Reunited, the two poets returned to their life together, to long walks throughout the city – 'Drury-Lane, White-Chapel, Pimlico, Angel, the City, Hyde-Park, etc., no longer hold any mystery for us' (*Corr.*, 301) – to their poetry, and to working on their English, especially reading (in May, Verlaine would tell Lepelletier that he had read all of Poe: 'je l'ai *tout lu* en english'; *Corr.*, 314). Verlaine's mood was drastically improved; as he wrote to Blémont in February, he was already looking forward

Félix Régamey, Rimbaud and Verlaine in a London Street, 1872.

to the summer, when he and Rimbaud would visit Brighton, and then maybe Scotland or Ireland.

On 24 March Verlaine signed up for a card for access to the reading room of the British Library (at the time, part of the British Museum). The following day Rimbaud followed suit, the nineteen-year-old signing his name to line 1,351 in the registry:

I have read the 'Directions respecting the Reading room',
And I declare that I am not under twenty-one years of age.

1351 Arthur Rimbaud 34 Howland street Fitzroy square W

There they would see other French exiles, including Vermersch, who was there nearly every morning. According to legend, Rimbaud's request to read the works of the Marquis de Sade was rejected.

Besides his reading, not many details are known of Rimbaud's second stay in London, but his time there and in Brussels no doubt contributed to his appreciation of the modern cityscape, which became an increasingly present backdrop for his poetry. Doubtless inspired by Baudelaire's city-based prose poems – written in the 1850s and 1860s but not published in their entirety until the poet's posthumous 1869 edition, which was edited by Charles Asselineau and none other than Théodore de Banville – Rimbaud put aside the dismantling of verse and drew on the fluidity and shape-shifting nature of the prose poem to describe the new urban space that he was discovering. It is hard not to think of the great post-Impressionist paintings of 1870s London while reading 'Les Ponts' (Bridges; *oc*, 300). The bridges evoked are of course spanning the Thames; at the same time, they stretch across all the modern cities; the feeling of alienation is the same along the Seine. Gone is any sort of lyricism: this example of Rimbaud's notion of objective poetry puts the scene in play in a manner that is practically devoid of human presence from the poem's opening:

Des ciels gris de cristal. Un bizarre dessin de ponts, ceux-ci droits, ceux-là bombés, d'autres descendant ou obliquant en angles sur les premiers, et ces figures se renouvelant dans les autres circuits éclairés du canal, mais tous tellement longs et légers que les rives chargées de dômes s'abaissent et s'amoindrissent.

Grey crystal skies. A bizarre pattern of bridges, some straight, some arched, others going down or veering off at angles to the first ones, and these shapes repeating themselves in other lighted circuits of the canal, but all of them so long and light that the banks heavy with domes are lowered and shrunken.

The perspective is a relative one: bridges are perched at angles to each other, they repeat each other, and they create shapes all by themselves. Faced with these newly formed shapes, the poetic subject is far from omniscient, and expressions of uncertainty abound: 'On distingue une veste rouge, peut-être d'autres costumes et des instruments de musique. Sont-ce des airs populaires, des bouts de concerts seigneuriaux, des restants d'hymnes publics?' (One can see a red jacket and perhaps other costumes and musical instruments. Are they popular tunes, bits of castle concerts, remnants of public hymns?). Amid unfamiliar surroundings, and unable to make them out clearly anyway, it is all too much to take in and so it becomes noise, essentially negating itself in the erasure of the last line: 'Un rayon blanc, tombant du haut du ciel, anéantit cette comédie' (A white ray, falling from the top of the sky, blots out this comedy).

But the poetic 'je' is not completely removed in these urban prose poems; at other times it is precisely his ability to see and describe the modernity around him that is itself poetic, as in 'Ville' (City; *oc*, 300–301):

Je suis un éphémère et point trop mécontent citoyen d'une
métropole crue moderne parce que tout goût connu a été éludé dans
les ameublements et l'extérieur des maisons aussi bien que dans le
plan de la ville. Ici vous ne signaleriez les traces d'aucun monument
de superstition. La morale et la langue sont réduites à leur plus
simple expression, enfin! Ces millions de gens qui n'ont pas besoin
de se connaître amènent si pareillement l'éducation, le métier et la
vieillesse, que ce cours de vie doit être plusieurs fois moins long que
ce qu'une statistique folle trouve pour les peuples du continent. Aussi
comme, de ma fenêtre, je vois des spectres nouveaux roulant à travers
l'épaisse et éternelle fumée de charbon, – notre ombre des bois, notre
nuit d'été! – des Erinnyes nouvelles, devant mon cottage qui est ma
patrie et tout mon cœur puisque tout ici ressemble à ceci, – la Mort

sans pleurs, notre active fille et servante, un Amour désespéré, et un joli Crime piaulant dans la boue de la rue.

I am an ephemeral and not-too-discontented citizen of a metropolis obviously modern because every known taste has been avoided in the furnishings and in the outsides of the houses as well as in the layout of the city. Here you would not discover the least sign of any monument of superstition. Morals and speech are reduced to their simplest expression, in short! These millions of people who have no need of knowing one another conduct their education, their trade, and their old age with such similarity that the duration of their lives must be several times shorter than, according to some insane statistics, is the case with the people on the continent. From my window, I see new ghosts rolling through thick, everlasting coal smoke, – our shadow in the words, our summer night! – new Furies in front of my cottage which is my country and my heart since everything here resembles it – Death without tears, our active daughter and servant, a desperate Love, and a pretty Crime crying in the mud of the street.

The perceptive reader can distinguish two voices inhabiting this deeply ironic text: the poet's and that of the object of the poet's criticism. Consistent with Rimbaud's desire to distinguish between poetic subject and object, in 'Ville' it is the poetic subject, the 'je' that – in addition to being 'un autre' – is set up as the object of ridicule. The first voice comes from a circumstantial inhabitant of a major metropolis, prudishly satisfied to find himself in such a modern city utterly devoid of taste. The position of the 'je' is reinforced by the 'vous' addressed in the second sentence, in which we learn that religion has surpassed naiveté and superstitions, just as the emotional interjection 'enfin!' continues to anchor the subject in the depiction of this cityscape where morals are free and language is direct. The irony comes through the poet's mockery: discrete at first, dominant at the end, it ridicules this apology for modernity. The city's plagues of industrial pollution, solitude and crime proliferate; it is hardly the place where one might be even somewhat content, and its lack of taste and flat expression are the site of violence, as with the Furies, the goddesses of vengeance. When the previously romantic and comforting summer night is aligned with the sinister shadow in the woods, the subject is very much situated in a menacing place, with no comfort to be found and no one to hear his 'Mort sans pleurs': what began as a faceless, tasteless city ends up with allegory and howls in the gutter.

Rimbaud wrote a number of other prose poems with similarly urban themes; while they are for the most part undated, they are most likely inspired by his time spent in major European cities. Such is the case for 'Métropolitain' (*oc*, 308–9), 'Promontoire' (*oc*, 310) and the two poems entitled 'Villes' (Cities), one beginning 'Ce sont des villes!' (They are cities!; *oc*, 301–2) and the other 'L'acropole officielle [. . .]' (The official acropolis'; *oc*, 303–4). But he had not given up on verse poetry completely, and just as he had already developed a knack for retaining some recognizable signposts of what he was mocking and tearing apart, his departure from verse poetry also resulted in the first two free-verse poems written in French, 'Marine' (*oc*, 307–8) and 'Mouvement' (*oc*, 312–13). In a manner that recalls the charge of his 'Voyant' – 'if what he brings back from *down there* has form, he gives form; if it is formless, he gives formlessness' – Rimbaud somehow lets verse poetry push out its last gasps as he steps past, moving towards something new.

Marine

Les chars d'argent et de cuivre –
Les proues d'acier et d'argent –
Battent l'écume, –

Soulèvent les souches des ronces –
Les courants de la lande,
Et les ornières immenses du reflux,
Filent circulairement vers l'est,
Vers les piliers de la forêt, –
Vers les fûts de la jetée,
Dont l'angle est heurté par des tourbillons de lumière.

Chariots of silver and copper – / Bows of steel and silver – / Beat the foam – / Raise up the stumps of bramble – / The currents of the moor / And the huge ruts of the ebb tide / Flow circularly towards the East, / Towards the pillars of the forest, – / Towards the poles of the pier, / Whose angle is struck by whorls of light.

Mouvement

Le mouvement de lacet sur la berge des chutes du fleuve,
Le gouffre à l'étambot,
La célérité de la rampe,
L'énorme passade du courant
Mènent par les lumières inouïes
Et la nouveauté chimique
Les voyageurs entourés des trombes du val
Et du strom.
Ce sont les conquérants du monde
Cherchant la fortune chimique personnelle;
Le sport et le comfort voyagent avec eux;
Ils emmènent l'éducation
Des races, des classes et des bêtes, sur ce Vaisseau.
Repos et vertige
À la lumière diluvienne,
Aux terribles soirs d'étude.

Car de la causerie parmi les appareils, – le sang, les fleurs, le feu, les
*   bijoux –*
Des comptes agités à ce bord fuyard,
– On voit, roulant comme une digue au-delà de la route hydraulique
*   motrice,*
Monstrueux, s'éclairant sans fin, – leur stock d'études; –
Eux chassés dans l'extase harmonique,
Et l'héroïsme de la découverte.

Aux accidents atmosphériques les plus surprenants
Un couple de jeunesse s'isole sur l'arche,
– Est-ce ancienne sauvagerie qu'on pardonne? –
Et chante et se poste.

The swaying motion on the bank of the river falls, / The chasm
at the sternpost, / The swiftness of the hand-rail, / The huge
passing of the current / Conduct by unimaginable lights /
And chemical newness / Voyagers surrounded by the
waterspouts of the valley / And the current. // They are
the conquerors of the world / Seeking a personal chemical
fortune; / Sports and comfort travel with them; / They take
the education / Of races, classes, and animals, on this Boat. /
Repose and dizziness / To the torrential light, / To the terrible
nights of study. // Far from the talk among the apparatus, –
blood, flowers, fire, jewels – / From the agitated accounts on
this fleeing deck, / – One can see, rolling like a dyke beyond
the hydraulic motor road, / Monstrous, illuminated endlessly,
– their stock of studies; / Themselves driven into harmonic
ecstasy / And the heroism of discovery. // In the most startling
atmospheric happenings / A youthful couple withdraws into the
archway, / – Is it an ancient coyness that can be forgiven? – /
And sings and stands guard.

To say that these poems marked something new would be an understatement. Even some ten years later, the journal that first published them did not know what to make of them. *La Vogue* typically printed prose in Roman characters and verse in italics, so when 'Marine' was published on 29 May 1886 it was set in roman – suggesting a prose poem – and in the 21 June issue 'Mouvement' appeared in italics, suggesting free verse.

The poems offer a modern cityscape at the confluence of the urban and the bucolic with conflicting and colliding shapes. Industrial beams cut through the metropolis at harsh new angles, with twists and turns and at a hurtling, arrhythmic pace, while a modern lexicon forges a new poetic idiom: these atmospheric, ecstatic and heroic scenes indeed herald a new future. And a new awareness: if it is not with optimism that in 'Mouvement' the couple 'chante et se poste', then it is at least with an eye to where they are going and what is to come. The future is less a function of the past than of the present, itself already irrevocably changed by the modernity all around.

Another aspect of the poems from this period is their ability to defy understanding, often with a final line that, recalling the sonnet's *chute*, turns the poem on its ear and requires that the entire scene be thought anew. 'Parade' (*oc*, 293–4) famously ends by sticking its tongue out at the readers and daring us to understand: 'J'ai seul la clef de cette parade sauvage' (I alone have the key to this wild circus). In 'H' (*oc*, 313–14), the poem's single paragraph is presented as an explanation of the opening line, 'Toutes les monstruosités violent les gestes atroces d'Hortense' (All forms of monstrosity violate the atrocious gestures of Hortense), only to end with the dare 'trouvez Hortense' (find Hortense).[6] More than towards an answer for the riddle, though, the ends of poems like 'H' and 'Parade' point readers towards a transcendence that exists beyond the language of the poem. Perhaps the point of the poem is to take its moment as a point of departure for something far beyond, the kind of future expression that is hinted at in the poem 'Départ' (*oc*, 296):

Assez vu. La vision s'est rencontrée à tous les airs.
Assez eu. Rumeurs des villes, le soir, et au soleil, et toujours.
Assez connu. Les arrêts de la vie. – Ô rumeurs et Visions!
Départ dans l'affection et le bruit neufs!

Seen enough. The vision met itself in every kind of air. / Had enough. Noises of cities in the evening, in the sunlight, and forever. / Known enough. The haltings of life. – Oh! Noises and Visions! / Departure into new affection and sound!

With their range of formal and thematic possibilities, these poems are a very heterogeneous bunch; and while at one point he had the intention of organizing them as a collection, Rimbaud did not see them published during his lifetime. He had thought of a title, though: according to Verlaine it was to be *Illuminations*. London clearly left its mark on this collection, as Verlaine used a phonetic spelling of the English pronunciation when he wrote the title: '*les Illuminécheunes*' (*Corr.*, 633), and in his preface to the poems Verlaine confirmed that Rimbaud had even intended to give his collection an English subtitle, 'Coloured Plates'.

While illuminating so much of the modern urban experience, the fascinating poems are able to draw from the cityscape without veering into autobiography; perhaps they offered a respite from the increasingly tortuous life with and without Verlaine, who remained torn between the young poet and the young wife. The early months of 1873 did not provide sufficient comfort, for in early April Verlaine left for the Continent, hoping to meet Mathilde and work out a solution that would not leave him entirely ruined. Mathilde would not listen, though, and as he feared reprisals for his Communard leanings – the police were keeping an eye on him, although much more for his private life in London than for his relatively tame Commune-era politics – he stayed outside France, with an aunt living in Jéhonville, in Luxembourg. From there he organized the publication of his next volume of poems, *Romances sans paroles* (1874); a significant departure from his earlier work, many of the poems give evidence to Rimbaud's influence. The third poem from the section 'Ariettes oubliées', which begins 'Il pleure dans mon cœur' (It is raining in my heart), bears an epigraph that Verlaine attributed to Rimbaud: 'Il pleut doucement sur la ville' (It is raining softly on the city).

Rather than stay alone in London, Rimbaud set off, too, and arrived the following week in Roche, at the family farm that his mother had inherited from the Cuif side of the family; his mother, brother and sisters were all there.[7] While not exactly a refuge of calm and warmth, it was a place to which he would return in the coming years. Although they were not living together, Rimbaud and Verlaine remained in contact and would meet up regularly in Bouillon, a small town in Belgium halfway between Charleville and Jéhonville. Delahaye would join them for these Sunday meetings, which Rimbaud referred to in a letter to Delahaye in which he expresses how little comfort he took from the family farm at Roche – which he called 'Laïtou':

Laïtou (Roche) (Canton d'Attigny) May 73

Dear friend, you can see my present life in this enclosed drawing.
     Oh Nature! Oh my mother!
     What a tough shit! and what monsters of innocence these peasants are! At night, to have a drink, you have to walk two leagues or more. *La Mother* has put me in this sad hole of a place.
     I don't know how to get out of it, but I will get out of it. I miss that vile Charlestown, The Universe [café], the Librar., etc . . . Yet I work quite steadily, I am writing little stories in prose, general title: *Livre païen* or *Livre nègre*. It is crazy and innocent. Oh innocence! innocence; innocence, innoc . . . plague!

[. . .]

I have nothing more to tell you, the contemplostasis of Nature completely absorbs me and fills my arse. I am yours, oh Nature, oh my mother!

I shake your hands, in the hope of a reunion that I am working on as much as possible.

I reopen my letter. Verlaine must have proposed to you that we meet on Sunday the 18th in Bouillon. I can't go. If you go, he will probably give you a few fragments of my prose, or his, to return to me.

Mother Rimb. will return to Charlestown sometime in June, no doubt, and I'll try to stay in that pretty town a little while.
[. . .]

I am absolutely thwarted. Not a book, not a bar within reach, not an incident in the street. How horrible this French countryside is! My fate depends on this book, for which I still have to invent a half-dozen atrocious stories. How can I invent atrocities here? I am not sending you any stories, although I already have three, *it costs too much!* That's all for now!

Rimb.

Stuck in some 'tough shit' and a 'hole', thanks to the peasants and 'la Mother'; while Charlestown is atrocious, it is nature that pushes him to neologisms in order to exorcize pathetic, insufficient language in 'la contemplostate de la Nature m'absorculant tout entier': first 'contemplostate' (contemplation and stasis) and then 'absorculer' (absorb and arse [*cul*]) and not just a partial 'absorcule' but a full one, completely ('tout entier'). Mother Nature is just as cold as 'la Mother', as we see in the mocking call 'I am yours' (Je suis à toi) that connects them both: it's as sincere as is the repeated claim of innocence. Note the letter's other repetition: 'Je ne sais comment en sortir: j'en sortirai pourtant' (I don't know how to get out of it, but I will get out of it). Despite not knowing how or where to go, he is adamant that he will find a way out. Surely the key to unlock the door to his future is this book he is writing, this book on which he depends so much. Whether pagan or 'nègre', this important book of atrocious stories would eventually bear the title *Une saison en enfer*.

Rimbaud's return to the Ardennes brought him some clarity. As had been the case during his childhood in Charleville (as well as his time in Paris, Brussels and London), boundaries, be they physical or poetic, sonorous or rhythmic, geographic or intellectual, would never be anything more than lines to step over, and they would always fail to contain him. And so back again he went: back to London with Verlaine, this time on the Great Eastern Railway steamer that left Antwerp on 27 May. They moved into 8 Great College Street, in Camden Town, where for three months they lived in two rooms on the top floor; it was a lively part of town that reminded Verlaine of Brussels. They lived rather well, thanks to money from Verlaine's mother and the income they earned from tuition, gained via advertisements they placed in newspapers:

LEÇONS de Français, Latin, Littérature, en français, par deux Gentlemen Parisiens; prix modérés. – Verlaine, 8 Great College-st., Camden-town

(The Echo, 11, 12, 13 June 1873)

LEÇONS DE FRANÇAIS, en français – perfection, finesses – par deux Gentlemen parisiens. – Verlaine, 8 Great College-street, Camden Town

(Daily Telegraph, 21 June)

Despite Verlaine's claim that they had put fifteen or so advertisements in the *Daily News*, *The Echo* and the *Daily Telegraph*, only one student showed up, agreeing to pay three shillings for each two-hour daily lesson. The money no doubt proved useful for going to see French operettas, which they did frequently. They also caught a glimpse of the Shah of Persia during his state visit on 18 June, took boat trips on the Thames and went for walks in the countryside, particularly past Highgate to the leafy suburbs beyond.

And yet, whatever hope they had had for a new beginning would quickly disappear, as they argued constantly and even fought physically. Verlaine was aware of the growing rumours about his homosexuality, and, as a police report on the milieu of exiled former Communards explains, the two poets were shunned for their increasingly erratic behaviour. Tensions mounted: Verlaine no doubt feared the deleterious effects of Mathilde's attempts at a legal separation should word of his life with Rimbaud make it back to Paris, and his increased drinking led to increased violence. One early July morning it all blew up: at the sight of Verlaine returning from the Camden fish market with some fresh fish – mackerel in one version of the story, herring in another – Rimbaud mocked his friend from the window, telling him that he looked ridiculous. Verlaine promptly entered, gathered his things and left for Brussels, hoping to lure Mathilde there for reconciliation. Letters immediately flew in all directions. From his room in the Grand Hôtel Liégeois (rue du Progrès), Verlaine sent letters of desperation to Paris – to Mathilde and to his mother, specifically – threatening suicide. From London, Rimbaud begged him to return:

Come back, come back, dear friend, my one friend, come back. I swear that I will behave. If I was surly with you, it was a joke. I couldn't stop. I am more repentant than I can say. Come back, everything will be forgotten. How terrible that you took that joke seriously. For two days now I haven't stopped crying. Come back. Be brave, dear friend. Nothing is lost. You have only to make the journey again. We will live here again courageously and patiently. Oh! I beg you. [. . .] But why didn't you come, when I signalled you to get off the boat? We lived together two years, to come to this moment. What are you going to do? If you don't want to come back here, do you want me to come to you?

Yes, I was in the wrong.
Oh you won't forget me, will you?
No, you can't forget me.
I still have you here.
Listen, answer your friend, aren't we to live together anymore?
Be brave. Answer me quickly.
I cannot stay here much longer.
Listen only to your good heart.
Quick, tell me if I should come to you.
Yours, all my life.

Rimbaud

[. . .]
Oh, come back. I am crying all the time. Tell me to come to you, and I will come, tell me, send me a wire – I have to leave Monday evening, where are you going what do you want to do.

As he was posting his letter and planning his departure by entrusting all of Verlaine's books and manuscripts to Vermersch, Rimbaud received a letter that Verlaine had written while the boat was taking him to Belgium. Verlaine's letter is lost, but the tone of Rimbaud's response makes clear what Verlaine had written:

Dear friend,
I have your letter dated '*At sea*'. You are wrong this time. First there is nothing positive in your letter: your wife is not coming or she will come in three months, or three years, who knows? As for dying, I know you. So, while waiting for your wife and your death, you are going to struggle, wander about, and annoy people. What, haven't you realized that our anger was wrong on both sides! But it is you who will be wrong in the end,

because, even after I called you back, you persisted in your false sentiments. Do you think life will be happier with others than it was with me? *Think about this!* – Oh! Certainly not! –

With me alone you can be free, and since I swear to you that I will behave in the future, I am sorry for all of my wrongdoing, that my mind is clear at last, that I am very fond of you, if you don't want to come back or don't want me to join you, you are committing a crime, and *you will repent for this for* LONG YEARS TO COME by *losing all freedom, and by more atrocious suffering perhaps* than any you have felt. After this, think of what you were before knowing me.

As for myself, I am not going back to my mother's. I am going to Paris, I will try to be gone by Monday. You will have forced me to sell all your clothes. I can do nothing else. They are not yet sold: they won't be taken from me until Monday morning. If you want to write to me in Paris, write to L[ouis] Forain, 289, rue Saint-Jacques for A. Rimbaud. He will know my address.

Believe me, if your wife comes back, I will not compromise you by writing to you, – I will never write.

The one true word is: come back, I want to be with you, I love you. If you heed this, you will show courage and sincerity.

Otherwise, I pity you. But I love you, I kiss you and we will see one another again. Rimbaud
8 Great Colle, etc. . . . until Monday evening, or Tuesday at noon, if you call for me.

The pleas to return to London fell on deaf ears, as did the letter that Verlaine received from Mme Rimbaud (for he had written to her as well) in which she implored him to be reasonable and not to do anything drastic. Waiting for the cast of characters to assemble and preparing his final act, Verlaine settled into the À la Ville de Courtrai hotel (rue des Brasseurs), where Verlaine's mother arrived, to be followed by Rimbaud on 8 July.

Two days later, Verlaine got up early and strolled through the city. In the St Hubert gallery he bought a 7-mm six-shooter, then settled into a café in the rue des Chartreux, where he filled the gun with bullets and his belly with liquor. Upon his return to the hotel at midday, he showed Rimbaud the gun and said that he planned to use it on all of them. When Rimbaud asked Verlaine's mother for the train fare back to France, Verlaine intervened and led his friend out to discuss it over some drinks at a café on the Grand-Place, where, not surprisingly, adding alcohol to an already heated situation did not improve matters, and their argument intensified.

Upon their return to the hotel at around two o'clock in the afternoon, Verlaine let Rimbaud enter their room first, stepped inside and locked the door behind him. The hotel room was not big; the two men were face to face, three metres from each other. Rimbaud stood with his back against the wall while Verlaine sat on a chair he had propped up against the door. In the ensuing argument, Verlaine drew his gun and shot twice: the first bullet hit Rimbaud in the left forearm and the second ricocheted off the wall and into the hearth. With Verlaine's mother they rushed to the Hôpital Saint-Jean for medical attention and then back to the hotel, where this time Rimbaud succeeded in getting Verlaine's mother to give him twenty francs so he could go back to France. On the way to the Brussels-Midi train station to see Rimbaud off, the two picked up their earlier dispute and Verlaine pulled his gun yet again, this time in public. Once shot, twice shy: Rimbaud got the attention of a police officer and denounced his friend. With rather damning evidence before him (a loaded gun in his hand, an accuser with a wrapped and bloody wound), Verlaine was immediately taken into police custody and charged; Rimbaud had to stay put to care for his wound and to give the police a statement. The examining magistrate of Brussels, Théodore t'Sterstevens, ordered a complete (and no doubt harrowing) physical examination that included a full body cavity search. In their report, Doctors Semal and Vleminckx concluded that Verlaine engaged in 'active and passive pederasty', exhibiting traces of 'more or less recent practices' (*JJL*, 617). After a week of convalescence that included the removal of the bullet a full week after he was shot, Rimbaud dropped all charges against Verlaine and left the hospital the next day, spending at least a few days in Brussels before finally getting on a train at Brussels-Midi and making his way back to Roche. He was probably already home by 8 August, when the Sixth Chamber of the Correctional Division of Brussels's Court of First Instance found Verlaine guilty, sentenced him to two years in prison and fined him two hundred francs; the verdict would be upheld by an appellate court a few weeks later.

With Verlaine rediscovering his faith in a prison cell in rural Mons and Rimbaud convalescing in Roche, the urban adventure had come to a screeching halt. Just as the two shots that tore through the idyllic canvas of 'Le Dormeur du val' had signalled the end of rural comfort for Rimbaud, so did the two shots in a Brussels hotel room mark the end of a decidedly different tableau. Somehow they had managed to anticipate 'L'amour est un oiseau rebelle' (Love is a rebellious bird), the famous aria from Georges Bizet's opera *Carmen* (1875): 'Si tu ne m'aimes pas, je t'aime; / Si je t'aime, prends garde à toi!' (If you do not love me, I love you; / If I love you, you'd best beware!). With trails of scorched earth behind them in Paris, Brussels and London, it was clear that the cities of Europe could no longer contain the two of them. Before Rimbaud could plan his next move, though, he needed to take some time to lick his wounds.

5

Wounds

Jadis, si je me souviens bien, ma vie était un festin où s'ouvraient tous les cœurs, où tous les vins coulaient.

Un soir, j'ai assis la Beauté sur mes genoux. – Et je l'ai trouvée amère. – Et je l'ai injuriée.

Je me suis armé contre la justice.

Long ago, if my memory serves me, my life was a banquet where everyone's heart was generous, and where all wines flowed. / One day, I sat Beauty down on my knee. – And I found her bitter. – And I insulted her. / I armed myself against justice.

It is with these lines from his untitled preface that Rimbaud begins *Une saison en enfer* (A Season in Hell). Insults have already been plentiful in Rimbaud's poetry: in his contributions to the *Album zutique*; in his criticisms of the bourgeoisie, the Church and the Second Empire; and in the soldiers' insults in 'Le Cœur supplicié'. Beauty was certainly not spared, if the 'Venus' / 'anus' rhyme is any indication. But it would be a mistake to take the 'atrocious stories' that make up the *Saison* as autobiography, some sort of strictly transparent commentary on his life and work up to that point. For despite some biographical elements they are so much more: they are elements of the narrator's catharsis as he returns from the abyss: 'Or, tout dernièrement m'étant trouvé sur le point de faire le dernier *couac*! J'ai songé à rechercher la clef du festin ancien, où je reprendrais peut-être appétit' (But recently, on the verge of giving my last *croak*, I thought of looking for the key to the ancient banquet where I might possibly recover my appetite). This new season is inscribed under a pact with the devil:

> *Ah! j'en ai trop pris: – Mais, cher Satan, je vous en conjure, une prunelle moins irritée! et en attendant les quelques petites lâchetés en retard, vous qui aimez dans l'écrivain l'absence des facultés descriptives ou instructives, je vous détache ces quelques hideux feuillets de mon carnet de damné.*

> Ah! I've taken too much on. Dear Satan, I beg you, show a less glaring eye! While waiting for the few small acts of cowardice still to come, for you who like in a writer an absence of descriptive or instructive faculties, I tear out these few hideous sheets from my notebook of the damned.[1]

As he sits and writes at the family farm in Roche, Rimbaud is indeed recovering from wounds in his poetic and personal life, both destroyed. Of course, Roche is not hell – not literally, at least, although one can imagine that Mme Rimbaud's maternal warmth provided comforts similar to those of the underworld – but his season of convalescence spent there involves taking stock of the past, finding a salve for his wounds, and eventually shedding some of what came before and moving on. *Une saison en enfer* offers these elements in all of their complexity: sounding their depths and going about them as they come, as the healing arrives.

And so he would go back to the beginning; the first section, entitled 'Mauvais sang' (Bad Blood'; *oc*, 247–53), divided into seven parts, traces a long anthropological history through the narrator's French lineage: characteristics related to body (eye colour, skull shape) and behaviour (flaying animals, scorching earth, idolatry). Recalling Rimbaud's declaration of being on strike in his letter to

Izambard from May 1871, the writer in 'Mauvais sang' is a worker like everyone else: 'J'ai horreur de tous les métiers. Maîtres et ouvriers, tous paysans, ignobles. La main à plume vaut la main à charrue. – Quel siècle à mains! – Je n'aurai jamais ma main' (I loathe all trades. All of them, foremen and workmen, are base peasants. A writer's hand is no better than a ploughman's. What a century of hands! I will never possess my hand). After the decimation of working-class Parisians at the end of the Paris Commune, what was the point of contributing to a society of production when even the commodification of poetry turns poets into workers? Heritage – which no doubt contributed heavily to Rimbaud, considering titles such as *Livre païen* and *Livre nègre* when he wrote to Delahaye in May – is heavy in these lines: 'Il m'est bien évident que j'ai toujours été de race inférieure' (It is very clear to me that I have always been part of an inferior race). He thus looks for what he would have been in earlier times and towards the future, made of science:

> *Qu'étais-je au siècle dernier: je ne me retrouve qu'aujourd'hui. [. . .]*
> *La race inférieure a tout couvert – le peuple, comme on dit, la raison;*
> *la nation et la science. . . . Géographie, cosmographie, mécanique,*
> *chimie! . . .*
> *La science, la nouvelle noblesse! Le progrès. Le monde marche!*
> *Pourquoi ne tournerait-il pas?*
> *C'est la vision des nombres. Nous allons à l'Esprit. C'est très*
> *certain, c'est oracle, ce que je dis. Je comprends, et ne sachant*
> *m'expliquer sans paroles païennes, je voudrais me taire.*

What was I in the last century? I recognize myself only today [. . .] The inferior race has covered everything: the people, as they say; reason, nation, and science. [. . .] Geography, cosmography, mechanics, chemistry! . . . / Science, the new nobility! Progress. The world marches on! Why shouldn't it turn back? / It is the vision of numbers. We are moving

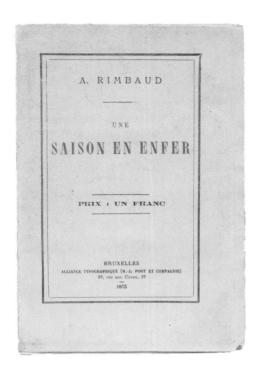

Arthur Rimbaud,
Une saison en enfer,
cover, 1873.

towards the *Spirit*. I tell you it is very certain, it is prophecy.
I understand it, and not knowing how to explain it without
using pagan words, I prefer to be silent.

The narration puts it all into question. What is race? Is it
French? Gallic? European? Moving forward involves stepping
out of the East/West dichotomy, only to return once again, having
moulted and taken on a new self: 'Ma journée est faite; je quitte
l'Europe. L'air marin brûlera mes poumons; les climats perdus me
tanneront. [. . .] Je reviendrai, avec des membres de fer, la peau
sombre, l'œil furieux: sur mon masque, on me jugera d'une race
forte. J'aurai de l'or: je serai oisif et brutal' (My day is done. I am
leaving Europe. The sea air will burn my lungs. Lost climates will

tan me. [. . .] I will come back with limbs of iron and dark skin and
a furious look: by my mask I will be judged as being from a strong
race. I will have gold: I will be lazy and brutal). But this return
ticket is not Rimbaud's any more than it is to or from Charleville;
it is the imagined voyage of the poet in search of an expression
that is neither pagan nor held back by Western knowledge. For
acknowledging our damnation is tantamount to acknowledging
that we cannot shake our bad blood:

> *Maintenant je suis maudit, j'ai horreur de la patrie [. . .]*
> *À qui me louer? Quelle bête faut-il adorer? Quelle sainte image*
> *attaque-t-on? Quels coeurs briserai-je? Quel mensonge dois-je tenir?*
> *– Dans quel sang marcher?*
> *Ô mon abnégation, ô ma charité merveilleuse! ici-bas, pourtant!*
> De profundis Domine, *suis-je bête!*

> Now I am damned, I loathe my country. [. . .] To whom can
> I sell myself? What a beast must I worship? What sacred image
> are we attacking? Whose heart shall I break? What lie should
> I tell? In whose blood shall I walk? [. . .] Oh my abnegation,
> oh my marvellous charity! Down here on earth, however!
> *De profundis Domine*, what a fool I am![2]

With every step backwards there is a potential step forward, and
despite the Enlightenment's failures there is hope for something
else: 'Oui, j'ai les yeux fermés à votre lumière. Je suis une bête, un
nègre. Mais je puis être sauvé' (Yes, my eyes are closed to your light.
I am a beast, a savage. But I can be saved). Clearly, though, salvation
for the narrator – and the poet, and the reader – exists beyond the
pagan language, defined and thus sullied by the West and its
horrors; perhaps it can be found in rhythms, beats and bodies:
'Connais-je encore la nature? me connais-je? – *Plus de mots*.
J'ensevelis les morts dans mon ventre. Cris, tambour, danse, danse,

danse, danse! Je ne vois même pas l'heure où, les blancs débarquant, je tomberai au néant. Faim, soif, cris, danse, danse, danse, danse!' (Do I know nature yet? Do I know myself? – *No more words*. I will bury the dead in my belly. Yells, drum, dance, dance, dance, dance! I can't even see the time when, the whites arriving, I will fall into the void. Hunger, thirst, dance, dance, dance, dance!). The narrator witnesses the Western appropriation of the world, and he wonders, 'Vite! est-il d'autres vies?' (Quick! Are there other lives?), for as he says as he nears his conclusion, 'Farce continuelle! Mon innocence me ferait pleurer. La vie est la farce à mener par tous' (An endless farce! My innocence would make me weep. Life is the farce we all play). The way forward is paved with more pain as the narrator is torn between a desire to move on beyond the punishment of his present condition, and not knowing where or how, ending in resignation. The first step in this season of healing is thus not accepting one's fate, nor trying to change it: just learning to live with it.

The next text, 'Nuit de l'Enfer' (Night in Hell; *oc*, 255–7), continues along these lines, at the moment of the narrator's death and entry into hell; it oscillates between the past – 'l'horloge de la vie s'est arrêtée tout à l'heure. Je ne suis plus au monde (Ah, the clock of life stopped just now. I am no longer in the world) – and a future poetic universe that the narrator can fill with whatever he wants:

Je vais dévoiler tous les mystères: mystères religieux ou naturels, mort, naissance, avenir, passé, cosmogonie, néant. Je suis maître en fantasmagories.

Écoutez! . . .

J'ai tous les talents! – Il n'y a personne ici et il y a quelqu'un: je ne voudrais pas répandre mon trésor. – Veut-on des chants nègres, des danses de houris? Veut-on que je disparaisse, que je plonge à la recherche de l'anneau? Veut-on? Je ferai de l'or, des remèdes.

Fiez-vous donc à moi, la foi soulage, guide, guérit.

I intend to unveil all mysteries: religious mysteries or those of nature, death, birth, the future, the past cosmogony, the void. I am a master of hallucinations. / Listen! . . . / I possess every talent! – There is no one here and there is someone. I would not like to spread around my treasure. – Do you want primitive songs or houri dances? Do you want me to disappear and dive after the *ring*? Do you? I will make gold and remedies. / So trust in me; faith relieves, guides, and cures.

The next section in the *Saison* offers what are perhaps the most direct autobiographical tones; entitled 'Délires' (Delirium), it is divided into two parts. 'Délires I' (*oc*, 259–62) bears two additional titles or subtitles: 'Vierge folle' (The Foolish Virgin) and 'L'Époux infernal' (The Infernal Bridegroom). The delirium itself is not as simple as madness in the personal and poetic realms, however: the French word *délire* can also suggest an un-reading ('dé-lire'), a text that is a combination of madness and an undoing of its own reading.[3] Clearly readers should be wary not to take such texts at face value.

And yet they often are. 'Délires I: Vierge folle. L'Époux infernal' tells the story from the perspective of the narrator's companion; the 'Vierge folle' is often taken to be Verlaine, who provides the portrait of his 'Époux infernal' in the form of a confession: 'Écoutons la confession d'un compagnon d'enfer' (Let us listen to the confession of a hell-mate). Their two monologues are intertwined, and thus Rimbaud creates a sort of indirect self-portrait, steps outside of himself to view himself as Other and consider how others perceive him. The 'Vierge folle' bemoans his involvement with the seductive youth:

> *Lui était presque un enfant . . . Ses délicatesses mystérieuses m'avaient séduite. J'ai oublié tout mon devoir humain pour le suivre. Quelle vie! La vraie vie est absente. Nous ne sommes pas au monde. Je vais où il va,*

il le faut. Et souvent il s'emporte contre moi, moi, la pauvre âme.
Le Démon! – C'est un Démon, vous savez, ce n'est pas un homme.
  *Il dit: 'Je n'aime pas les femmes. L'amour est à réinventer, on
le sait.'*

He was almost a child . . . His mysteriously delicate feelings
had seduced me. I forgot all my human duty to follow him.
What a life! Real life is absent. We are not in the world.
I go where he goes; I have to. And often he flies into a rage
at *me, poor me.* The Demon! He is a demon, you know. *He
is not a man.* / He said: 'I do not like women. Love is to be
reinvented, that is clear.'

This section is replete with themes common to the rest of *Une
saison en enfer*: distrust of conventional love; fascination with crime;
interest in gold and far-off lands; and representation of self in many
of its possible stances and poses. The narrator returns for a final
exclamation, 'Drôle de ménage!' (strange couple!).
  'Délires II: Alchimie du verbe' (Alchemy of the Word; *oc,* 263–9)
details the poetic side of the supposed autobiography, as the narrator
repudiates his past poetic attempts and laments his dashed hopes:

À moi. L'histoire d'une de mes folies.
  *Depuis longtemps je me vantais de posséder tous les paysages
possibles, et trouvais dérisoire les célébrités de la peinture et de la
poésie moderne.*
  *J'aimais les peintures idiotes, dessus de portes, décors, toiles de
saltimbanques, enseignes, enluminures populaires; la littérature
démodée, latin d'église, livres érotiques sans orthographe, romans
de nos aïeules, contes de fées, petits livres de l'enfance, opéras vieux,
refrains niais, rythmes naïfs.*
  *Je rêvais croisades, voyages de découvertes dont on n'a pas de
relations, républiques sans histoires, guerres de religion étouffées,*

révolutions de mœurs, déplacements de races et de continents: je
croyais à tous les enchantements.

J'inventai la couleur des voyelles! – A noir, E blanc, I rouge, O bleu,
U vert. – Je réglai la forme et le mouvement de chaque consonne, et,
avec des rythmes instinctifs, je me flattai d'inventer un verbe poétique
accessible, un jour ou l'autre, à tous les sens. Je réservais la traduction.

It is my turn. The story of one of my follies. / For a long time
I had boasted of having every possible landscape, and found
laughable the celebrated names of painting and modern poetry.
/ I liked stupid paintings, door panels, stage sets, backdrops for
acrobats, signs, popular engravings, old-fashioned literature,
Church Latin, erotic books with bad spelling, novels of our
grandmothers, fairy tales, little books from childhood, old
operas, ridiculous refrains, naive rhythms. / I dreamed of
crusades, of unrecorded voyages of discovery, of republics with
no history, of hushed-up religious wars, revolutions in customs,
displacements of races and continents: I believed in every kind of
witchcraft. / I invented the colour of the vowels! *A* black, *E* white,
I red, *O* blue, *U* green. – I regulated the form and movement of
each consonant, and, with instinctive rhythms, I prided myself
on inventing a poetic language accessible, some day, to all the
senses. I reserved translation rights.

In addition to this reference to 'voyelles', he provides other
examples of the kinds of verse poetry that he rejects by
inserting into his repudiation seven poems, sometimes slightly
modified from earlier known versions: 'Larme', 'Bonne pensée
du matin', 'Chanson de la plus haute tour', 'Fêtes de la faim',
'Le loup criait sous les feuilles' [. . .]', 'Éternité' and 'Ô saisons,
ô châteaux [. . .]'. In addition, his comments on his own
disappointments include images that echo passages in
Illuminations, allowing us to date at least some of those

poems – including 'Enfance ɪɪ' and 'Soir historique' – as having been written prior to April–August 1873.

It is all further complicated by this section's last line, which suggests a new way forward: 'Cela s'est passé. Je sais aujourd'hui saluer la beauté' (That is over. Today I can greet beauty). If sitting Beauty down on a knee and insulting her are in the past, what is in the future? Are the *Illuminations* the model of a future poetics, the culmination of Rimbaud's project of objective poetry? Certainly not, since at least some of them are referenced in these passages that the narrator is eager to leave behind. He might be able to greet beauty, but he is still coming to grips with the poetic detritus he has strewn about. And perhaps it is not all that bad: even if he is in hell, he is only there for a season; this purgatory is merely a transitional step, somewhere between hate and love, torture and joy, drunkenness and clarity; between the values and faith of the West and the harsh measures undertaken to expose and question them in the light of day. The strength of *Une saison en enfer* – evident in the narrator's swaying positions and postures, and the terse and tense language – lies in the irreducible contradiction between these two poles. Stuck in the Christian tradition, there is no choosing between heaven and hell; both are merely moral constructions, places along the spiritual topography unfurled before him. Rather than the two extremes meeting each other, it is more a question of good and bad being equally constructed, equally hollow, equally false: beauty, charity and wisdom are the same as Satan, revolt and violence. The way out is through the alchemy of poetic language and the madness, comedies and hallucinations it brings to life.

The remaining sections of the *Saison* continue along similar lines: 'L'Impossible' (*oc*, 271–3) offers some thoughts about escaping from hell, only to give up somewhat in 'L'Éclair' (Lightning; *oc*, 275–6) before arriving at a sort of conclusion in 'Matin' (Morning; *oc*, 277). There the narrator, breathless and speechless, sees the light at the end of the tunnel: 'Moi, je ne puis pas plus m'expliquer que le mendiant avec ses continuels *Pater* et *Ave Maria. Je ne sais plus parler!* Pourtant, aujourd'hui, je crois avoir fini la relation de mon enfer. C'était bien l'enfer; l'ancien, celui dont le fils de l'homme ouvrit les portes' (I can no more explain myself than the beggar with his endless *Paters* and *Ave Marias. I have forgotten how to speak!* Yet, today, I think I have finished the story of my hell. It was really hell; the old one, the one whose gates were opened by the son of man'). The season is over, and the final section, 'Adieu' (*oc*, 279–80), announces a change of seasons, exclaiming, 'L'automne déjà!' (Autumn already!) with its first words to herald a new beginning. The narrator is stronger for this journey, arriving at a new clarity, as this section, and *Une saison en enfer*, ends on this note:

> *Oui, l'heure nouvelle est au moins très sévère.*
>
> *Car je puis dire que la victoire m'est acquise: les grincements de dents, les sifflements de feu, les soupirs empestés se modèrent. Tous les souvenirs immondes s'effacent. Mes derniers regrets détalent, – des jalousies pour les mendiants, les brigands, les amis de la mort, les arriérés de toutes sortes. – Damnés, si je me vengeais!*
>
> *Il faut être absolument moderne.*
>
> *Point de cantiques: tenir le pas gagné. Dure nuit! le sang séché fume sur ma face, et je n'ai rien derrière moi, que cet horrible arbrisseau!... Le combat spirituel est aussi brutal que la bataille d'hommes; mais la vision de la justice est le plaisir de Dieu seul.*
>
> *Cependant c'est la veille. Recevons tous les influx de vigueur et de tendresse réelle. Et à l'aurore, armés d'une ardente patience, nous entrerons aux splendides villes.*
>
> *Que parlais-je de main amie! un bel avantage, c'est que je puis rire des vieilles amours mensongères, et frapper de honte ces couples menteurs, – j'ai vu l'enfer des femmes là-bas; – et il me sera loisible de* posséder la vérité dans une âme et un corps.
>
> avril–août, 1873.

Yes, the new hour is at least very harsh. / For I can say that victory is mine: the gnashing of teeth, the hissing of fire, the reeking sighs abate. All filthy memories fade out. My last regrets scamper off: envy of beggars, brigands, friends of death, backwards creatures of all sorts. – You who are damned, what if I avenged myself? / We must be absolutely modern. / No hymns. I must hold what has been gained. Hard night! The dried blood smokes on my face, and I have nothing behind me except that horrible tree! . . . A spiritual battle is as brutal as a battle of men; but the vision of justice is the pleasure of God alone. / However this is the vigil. Let us welcome all the influxes of vigor and real tenderness. And, at dawn, armed with ardent patience, we will enter magnificent cities. / What was I saying about a friendly hand? One fine advantage is that I can laugh at old lying loves and strike with shame those lying couples – I saw the hell of women down there – and I shall be free *to possess truth in one soul and one body*.

The narrator will forge ahead with this new truth in harmony of mind and body, and he will go it alone. For all the repudiation of the past that Rimbaud includes in the *Saison*, he arrives at an optimism: 'Adieu' is an offering to God ('à Dieu'), leaving behind Satan and hell, and with them there is at least a suggestion of leaving the West.

Unlike so many other parts of his poetic work, *Une saison en enfer* was a finished product that Rimbaud created and oversaw from beginning to end. Drafts of the few existing manuscript pages (in the collection of the Bibliothèque nationale de France) show the extent to which he worked on these texts before he brought them to 37 rue au Choux in Brussels.[4] There, J. Poot was director of the Alliance typographique, which published the volume *à compte d'auteur*: it was commonplace for poets to pay for their work to be published. Rimbaud picked up a few copies and had seven of them sent to friends (including one copy sent to Verlaine). The book on which his fate depended was met with total silence: not even the slightest mention in the press has been found, and the remaining stock was left with the publisher – no doubt because the author did not have the means to pay for them. After his death, Rimbaud's sister Isabelle claimed that her brother had had the remaining copies sent to him, whereupon he burned them in front of her. That story would prove false – it was one of her many fabrications about her brother's life – as 425 copies were found in a Brussels warehouse in 1901 by the lawyer and bibliophile Léon Losseau.[5]

When Rimbaud wrote from 'Laïtou' to Delahaye in May 1873, not only did he refer to the 'little stories in prose' that he was writing but he mentioned 'a few fragments of my prose' that were already done, and in Verlaine's possession. Are these texts part of the same project? Could these be the poems by Rimbaud that Verlaine had mentioned in a letter the previous year to Lepelletier, when he referred to 'ten or so letters from Rimbaud containing verses and prose poems' (*Corr.*, 268)? Given the number of citations of and references to poems in both verse and prose in 'Alchimie du verbe', it is likely that some of the prose poems from *Illuminations* were written before and some after the April–August 1873 dates of the *Saison*. To be sure, they are different works: one conceived of by the author as a complete volume, with an internal order and logic that guides the reader through its various twists and turns; the other, a group of manuscripts without a particular structure or logic keeping the disparate pieces together, whether in order of pages or even dates of composition.

It is difficult to know for certain which poems from *Illuminations* were written after *Une saison en enfer*, although the first line of 'Après le Déluge' (After the Flood; *OC*, 289–90), the poem that traditionally opens *Illuminations*, suggests that a new poetic universe is in store: 'Aussitôt après que l'idée du Déluge se fut rassise [. . .]' (As soon as the idea of the Flood had subsided). Beyond the urban scenes in other poems, the poetic landscape at times tends to be otherworldly;

such is the case in 'Aube' (Dawn; *oc*, 306), with its embrace of
summer ('J'ai embrassé l'aube d'été'; I have held the summer dawn
in my arms) and its call for a new poetic moment underscored by
the use of the German word for waterfall – 'Je ris au wasserfall
blond' (I laughed at the blonde wasserfall) – to signal that French
would no longer be enough.

Similarly extraterrestrial is 'Barbare' (Barbarian; *oc*, 309–10),
which begins with the contradiction between the pre-civilized state
suggested in the title (itself practically a pre-linguistic stammering
of two sounds, *bar bar*) and the poem's setting: 'Long after the days
and the seasons, and the people and the countries'. Unlike the time
stamp at the end of 'Matinée d'ivresse' (Morning of Drunkenness;
oc, 297–8) – 'Voici le temps des *Assassins*' (Behold the age of
Murderers) – the poetic landscape in 'Barbare' presents a time
and place so unfamiliar that nothing is recognizable. In the next
line, which doubles as the poem's refrain – 'Le pavillon en viande
saignante sur la soie des mers et des fleurs arctiques; (elles n'existent
pas)' (The flag of red meat over the silk of the seas and the Arctic
flowers; (they don't exist.)) – the strange juxtaposition of objects
reads like synaesthesia on acid. The poet-magician breaks the rules
and shows us his tricks; objects can be created out of thin air and in
the blink of an eye, and erased just as easily. Such is the case of the
emotions that poetry conveys, here in the form of outbursts: 'Oh
happiness, oh world, oh music! And there: forms, sweating, hair,
and eyes, floating'. Beyond the subjective/objective binary, here
poetry emerges as something elemental, dislocated from subject,
narrator, poet or body: 'And white tears, boiling – oh happiness!
– and the feminine voice coming from the depths of the volcanoes
and the arctic grottoes. The flag . . .'. The refrain's return and its
ellipsis signal that the barbarian–civilized cycle will continue:
creating and negating, forever. The endless, infinite quality of some
aspects of Rimbaud's post-verse poetry recalls this passage from
A Midsummer Night's Dream, in which Bottom explains his dream:

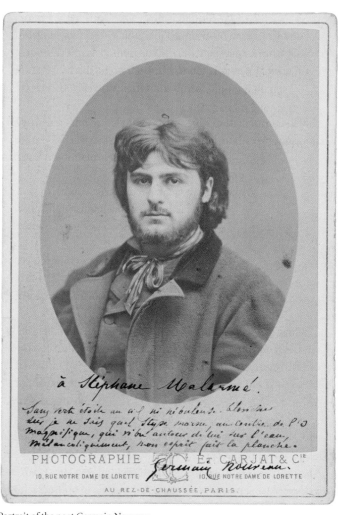

Portrait of the poet Germain Nouveau.

I have had a most rare vision. I have had a dream, past the wit of man to say what dream it was. Man is but an ass, if he go about t'expound this dream. Methought I was – there is no man can tell what. Methought I was, and methought I had – but man is but a patch'd fool, if he will offer to say what methought I had. The eye of man hath not heard, the ear of man hath not seen, man's hand is not able to taste, his tongue to conceive, nor his heart to report, what my dream was. I will get Peter Quince to write a ballad of this dream: it shall be called 'Bottom's Dream', because it hath no bottom [. . .] (Act IV, Scene 1)

The bottomless dreamscapes of the *Illuminations* continue in the poem entitled, precisely, 'Bottom' (*oc*, 313), which begins by rejecting reality, too prickly for the narrator's noble character. Appearing as bird, a bear and then an ass, he mutates through an endless sequence of colourful utopias; there is no reality to hold sway or offer purchase: this poetic dream, too, 'hath no bottom'.

Just as endless would be Rimbaud's movement. Recovered from his gunshot wound, he went again to Paris, no doubt in the hopes that one new *Saison* could mark the start of another. No luck: he hadn't anticipated the extent to which he had become *persona non grata* among the poets he had abused, either verbally or physically. He did manage to find one poet who would still talk to him: Germain Nouveau. Under the pseudonym P. Néouvielle, Nouveau had published his first poem in November 1872 in *La Renaissance littéraire et artistique*, a short-lived journal edited by the former Vilains Bonshommes member and *Coin de table* stander Émile Blémont. In short order Nouveau gained entry into several of the small literary circles that were active in Paris, including 'les Vivants', the tiny group – composed of Maurice Bouchor and erstwhile Zutistes Jean Richepin, Raoul Ponchon and Paul Bourget – that had the *Album zutique* in its possession. Nouveau was thus intimately familiar with the Zutistes and had doubtless heard all about Rimbaud by the time they met in late 1873. How long Rimbaud managed to stay in the capital is unknown – it is likely that he returned to Charleville for winter – but in March 1874 he and Nouveau were living in London, giving French lessons in their rented room at 178 Stamford Street, Waterloo.

The following month they crossed the Waterloo Bridge (the Northern Line wouldn't be an option until 1890) and registered in the British Museum's reading room. Rimbaud must have been in a playful mood when he signed the Registry, since he added 'Joseph' to his Christian name:

> I have read the 'Directions respecting the Reading room',
> *And I declare that I am not under twenty-one years of age.*

> 2336   Jean-Nicolas-Joseph-Arthur Rimbaud. 178 Stamford Street, Waterloo Road SE

> I have read the 'Directions respecting the Reading room',
> *And I declare that I am not under twenty-one years of age.*

> 2337   Marie Bernard Germain Nouveau. 178 Stamford Street, Waterloo Road

While they were in London, Nouveau began to study English, while Rimbaud made lists of vocabulary words so as to polish the language that he already knew well: archives hold nine sheets of paper with nearly five hundred words or expressions filling both sides. To say that his lexicon was becoming more specialized would be an understatement;[6] lists of words detailed raising animals, training pigeons, hunting, horticulture, cricket and heraldry, including:

butter boat
scimitar – self-cocking
fiscals – reversible rug
over moulting – hunting bridles
high shouldered canaries – steel bits
winder – body roller. Knee caps
mealy – saddletree. girths. stirrup irons
good spangles – hunting crop and thong
tabby kitten – masks and foils x
good hutch – enchanted wand
kestrel hawk – muzzle loader
dormice – fowling-piece
early hatched – air pump, wad punch
hand reared – snap action
half-lop buck. good hiller, small bore
evenly marked – wigs and tights
lop ears. – silver ferrule. (meerschaum)
– cuckoo clock – tea cosy violee [*sic*]
Hall-bracket clock
on jean.
half-tester bedstead
bow front.
three draw telescope
dancing holland
crumb cloth
lace and gimp
pinafores.
ends full and crimpled. – throatlet
grebe collarette. – silver appliques
never taken out of parcel – a spray
scalloped. – insertion for petticoat
crochet lappets, tips
wideawake shape – dressing dolls.

And, on another page:

frosted silver letters
flat straw letters
Holly berry. Wagga wagga berry
Hardy blue
suited for forcing
training roots
crimson clove
spikes of bloom
quilled variety.
seedlings.
yield wonderfully, (trees)
–
loose beads
garnet bracelet
cairngorm
paste diamont
chain, bar, and whistle – swivel
curb, long link
plated snake
Dogs: good ranger. Very staunch
drops to hand or shot
fast ranger. – lady's lap dog
over distemper – colley dog
Retriever, clumber. Yard dog
  French Beagles.
well broken. – good fencer
tender mouthed. Good pedigree
ears cut up like darts
Punishing head – barred head
keep well to heel – worth his weight . . .
fine close coat:

perfect drop ears – fine whip tail
spot on tern, on rump
whelped in J expected in pup perfect in points and markings
nicely marked and pencilled

By the time Nouveau moved out in early May – he would leave London soon thereafter – he had helped Rimbaud recopy some of the poems from *Illuminations*; the manuscripts for some (including 'Métropolitain' and 'Villes' ('L'acropole officielle [. . .]')) exist only in Nouveau's handwriting. Rimbaud, too, would be on the move; on 9, 10 and 11 June he placed an advertisement in *The Echo*, requesting that replies be sent to his new address, in a street that is today known as Maple Street: 'A young Parisian – speaks *passablement* – requires conversations with English gentlemen; his own lodgings, p.m. preferred. – Rimbaud, 40 London-st., Fitzroy-sq., W'. The advert didn't generate much interest, and without success it was no doubt hard to earn a living. Undernourished, Rimbaud was admitted to a hospital towards the end of June, and he sent a letter to Charleville in early July; one can only imagine how low he must have felt to turn to his mother for comfort. But comfort did come – or at least 'la Mother' did, with his sixteen-year-old sister Vitalie in tow. They stayed in a nearby rooming house at 12 Argyle Square, King's Cross, a half-hour walk from his flat in London Street. During their first few days in London, Rimbaud showed them around the city that by now he knew quite well: the Tower of London, Westminster, Trafalgar Square, the National Gallery, St Paul's Cathedral, and even gaslit Tower Subway, which Rimbaud and Verlaine had used to pass under the Thames two years earlier.

Tourism soon ended, and Rimbaud returned to long days reading and working on his English in the British Library reading room and looking for work. It paid off, for on 11 July he received a letter with three job offers (none of which he accepted, much to the disappointment of homesick Vitalie). Finally in late July

Rimbaud accepted a job that would require his leaving London;
he helped his mother and sister plan their return to France. Where
he worked in August, September and October is unclear, but by
November he was in Reading, working as an assistant to a certain
Camille Le Clair, who offered classes in his residence twice daily.
The job and the county town's already healthy reputation for beer,
bulbs and biscuits were apparently not enough, for he placed a
new advert in *The Times* on 7 and 9 November:

A PARISIAN (20), of high literary and linguistic attainments,
excellent conversation, will be glad to ACCOMPANY A GENTLEMAN

(artists preferred), or a family wishing to travel in southern
or eastern countries. Good references. – A.R., No. 165,
King's Road, Reading.

Without success, he returned to Charleville in late December, only
to be off again; with some glimmers of hope for earning his keep
with languages, he turned to German, which he began studying
in earnest. The immersive environment he had enjoyed in England
must have taught him something about language acquisition, for in
February 1875 the poet who had written 'The same bourgeois magic
wherever the trunk sets us down!' in 'Soir historique' (*Illuminations*)
filled his small trunk with a few belongings and some money from
his mother and headed southeast to Stuttgart. Upon his arrival,
after a possible stay with the art historian and professor Wilhelm
Lübke in a four-storey building at Urbanstrasse 34, he rented a
room at Hasenbergstrasse 7, in a boarding-house run by the retired
pastor Ernst Rudolf Wagner.

Early in Rimbaud's stay in Stuttgart he would see Verlaine
in person one last time. Verlaine had been released from prison
on 16 January, some six months early, for good behaviour. During
his incarceration his thoughts led to a newfound religious fervour
that would be a recurring theme in his poetry, in a volume written
while in prison entitled *Cellulairement* and in later volumes such
as *Sagesse* (1880), *Jadis et naguère* (1884) and *Parallèlement* (1889).
Hoping to convince Rimbaud to follow a similar path – Verlaine
had proposed 'Aimons-nous en Jésus!' (Let us love each other
in Jesus), according to Delahaye – they met in the Black Forest
near Stuttgart. As Rimbaud explained in a letter to Delahaye,
the meeting did not go as Verlaine had planned:

> Verlaine arrived here the other day, rosary in hand . . . After
> three hours he had renounced his god and made the 98 wounds
> of Our Lord bleed. He stayed for two and a half days and was

very sensible; upon my remonstration he retraced his steps back to Paris and, from there, went to finish studying *over there, on the island*. (*oc*, 376)

The emphasized reference to the island ('*là-bas dans l'île*') is typically Rimbaldian for its multiple resonances. Of course, it refers to England, where he and Verlaine had lived and to where Verlaine would return. It was also lifted from the refrain by a poem by Banville of 1869 entitled 'Ballade de Victor Hugo, père de tous les rimeurs'; the poem's three stanzas and its coda end with the same line: 'Mais le père est là-bas, dans l'île'. Little is known of their two and a half days together, but we do know that it is at this time that Verlaine gave some poems composed in Mons to Rimbaud, who reciprocated with the poems that would become *Illuminations*. Verlaine was to give them to Nouveau, who would have them published in Belgium (according to Verlaine this handoff was mostly evidence of Rimbaud's frugality, although the amount he would save would not be more than a few francs).

With Verlaine out of the picture, Rimbaud picked up where he left off: lists of foreign vocabulary words, advertisements in newspapers. In the *Schwäbische Kronik* of 7 March he offered to exchange French courses for German courses:

Ein Pariser, 20 J. alt, wäre geneigt, mit Lernbegierigen Personen die deutsche Sprache gegen die französische zu studiren.
Briefe an
A. Rimbaud
Hasenbergstr. 7, Stuttgart.

[A twenty-yr.-old Parisian would be interested in studying German in exchange for French lessons for those who are eager to learn it. / Letters to A. Rimbaud, Hasenbergstrasse 7, Stuttgart.]

A week later he had a new address: Marienstrasse 2, where, he explained to his family, he had a large, furnished room in the city centre for ten florins with service included, and the possibility of full pension for 60 francs per month. The financial realities of life were starting to add up, and he needed to make whatever money his mother would send him last as long as possible (or at least demonstrate frugality in the hope that his line of credit would remain in good stead). In April Rimbaud wrote to Verlaine, via Delahaye, and tried to convince his former partner to send him a hundred francs for the English that Rimbaud had taught him in London, in exchange for Rimbaud's discretion regarding their relationship. No doubt still hurting from the rejection in Stuttgart, Verlaine wrote to Delahaye and attempted to clarify 'la question Rimbaud':

Let's clear up the Rimbaud question. First of all, I did everything not to quarrel with him. The last word of my last letter to him was: 'Cordially'. And I explained in detail my arithmetical reasons for not sending him money. He responded: 1) with insolence enlivened with obscure threats of extortion; 2) with complicated calculations that somehow made it good business for me to give him the sum in question. – Without including a missive written in a drunkard's gibberish, which I think was trying to suggest that future letters could exist unless I *cough up money*, and if not then *zut*! – In a word, speculation on my former silliness, on my guilty madness from not long enough ago of *wanting* to live only through him and his breath; – plus the insufferable rudeness of a child whom I spoiled too much and who pays me back – oh logic! oh justice in all things! – with the most *stupid* ingratitude. For didn't he kill the goose that laid the golden eggs, really?

But *I did not quarrel*. I'm waiting for apologies, without promises, and if someone sulks, well then let him sulk! Is this not well reasoned? After all, he didn't do me a great service, the philomath! (*Corr.*, 390)

The philomath was already looking beyond; he told Delahaye that at his current pace he would be done learning German in two months and that, while he would only be staying chez Wagner for another week, Delahaye should write back to general delivery, Stuttgart. He wasn't yet ready to leave Stuttgart.

As for Verlaine, he would indeed go over there, to the island. In May he crossed paths with Nouveau, who had done his own travelling since he left Rimbaud (Belgium, the Netherlands, then back to London to work on his English). Verlaine dutifully entrusted Rimbaud's poems to him, and the project of publishing *Illuminations* inched forward. Not only were some of the manuscripts in Nouveau's hand, but the elder poet no doubt sensed that he was not the best person to see it through; he was still trying to figure out how to stanch the bleeding of the '98 wounds of Our Lord', and how to heal all the other wounds that Rimbaud had left in his life.

6

Worlds

With his two former travelling companions to the north, in
England, Rimbaud prepared to go south. Running low on cash
and with no more money forthcoming from Verlaine, the spoilt
child sold his trunk. Rimbaud had never let a lack of money limit
his travel plans; after a train to the Swiss border he forged ahead on
foot, crossing the Alps via the Gotthard Pass and arriving in Milan
exhausted. A calling card gives his address as piazza del Duomo 39,
third floor; there a wine merchant's widow who had lost her own
son the previous year took in the weary 21-year-old and took care of
him for a few weeks. As a show of thanks, the poet sent for his own
copy of *Une saison en enfer* and gave it to her. Once he was strong
enough to head further south, he did: to Livorno, a port on the west
coast of Tuscany. He wanted to make it to one of the Aegean islands,
where the former Zutiste Henri Mercier was part-owner in a soap
manufacturing company. The trip to the Cyclades went via Siena,
and then Brindisi, and Rimbaud quickly understood that there was
always work to be had along international shipping routes. Work for
someone who could speak the language, anyway, and so Rimbaud
pressed on: after Latin and Greek in Charleville, English in London,
German in Stuttgart, now Italian in Milan. Two years later he would
reasonably boast of his ability to speak English, German, French,
Italian and Spanish (*oc*, 466), and a dozen years after their last
meeting in Stuttgart Verlaine would still remember his friend as
a 'prodigieux linguiste' (*opc*, 801).

But he didn't make it to see Mercier; on the way to Siena he was overcome with sunstroke. The French consulate in Livorno put him up in a hotel for a few days, gave him pocket money and repatriated him to Marseille. Once there, his health being no better, he spent his first visit to France's oldest city in hospital, recovering. While he waited for his body to regain its strength, he decided to sign up as a mercenary to fight alongside the Carlists in support of Don Carlos's claim to the throne; as Delahaye explained it to Verlaine, Rimbaud figured that it would be a quick way to learn Spanish. Referring to this decision to enlist, Verlaine sent Delahaye a mocking poem entitled 'Ultissima verba' (Very Last Word; *Corr.*, 424): yet another reference to Hugo, whose poem 'Ultima verba' had appeared in *Les Châtiments*. Playfully poking fun at Rimbaud's ability to consume great quantities of absinthe and foreign languages, this very last word – a *dixain* signed 'F. C.' in the Zutique style, to insist on its imitation of François Coppée – also brings in Rimbaud's mother ('la *daromphe*'), Cros and Cabaner ('Tronche'):

> *Épris d'absinthe pure et de philomathie*
> *Je m'emmerde et pourtant au besoin j'apprécie*
> *Les théâtres qu'on peut avoir et les Gatti.*
> *'Quatre-vingt-treize' a des beautés et c'est senti*
> *Comme une merde, quoi qu'en disent Cros et Tronche*
> *Et l'Acadême où les Murgers boivent du ponche.*
> *Mais plus de bleus et la daromphe m'a chié.*
> *C'est triste et merde alors et que foutre? J'y ai*
> *Pensé beaucoup. Carlisse? Ah! non, c'est rien qui vaille*
> *À cause de l'emmerdement de la mitraille!*
>   *F. C.*

In love with pure absinthe and philomathy / I'm bored shitless and yet when the need arises I appreciate / The theatre halls that one can enjoy on the Gatti. / *Ninety-three*[1] has some beauties and

yet it smells / Like shit, despite the comments from Cros and
Tronche / And the Acadêm' where the Murgers drink ponch. /
But no more smokes and *la daromphe* shits on me. / It's sad and
damn it and what the fuck to do? I have / Thought about it a lot.
Carlists? Oh, no, it's not worth it / Because of the problem of
hails of bullets!

It is hard to fault Rimbaud for an aversion to 'la mitraille'; he had
already been shot at, after all. Instead of serving, he took the money
and left. Then – according to Nouveau, who heard the news from
Louis Forain – he was in Paris in late July, living with Mercier and
Cabaner. By late August he was back in Charleville. With no dock
work to be found along the sleepy Meuse, he turned his attention
to other ideas: his military service and his baccalauréat exam, after
which he could go to the université Polytechnique. (Such was his
plan, anyway; he didn't realize that, as he had just turned 21, he had
just exceeded the Polytechnique's age limit for incoming students.)
He also spent his days at the piano that Mme Rimbaud had rented
for him, taking lessons and practising day and night.

When Delahaye told him about Rimbaud's thoughts of heading
towards the sciences, Verlaine wondered who had given such advice
to 'Homais' – a mocking reference to the pharmacist in *Madame
Bovary* who had scientific pretensions, and one of Verlaine's many
nicknames for Rimbaud, which also included 'Chose' (Thing),
'l'Homme' (Man), 'l'Autre' (the Other) and 'l'Œstre' (the parasitic
bot-fly, from the family Oestridae). Verlaine then asked Delahaye to
send any poems in his possession by 'l'Être' (the Being) – another
nickname, nearly identical in pronunciation to 'l'Œstre' – to which
Delahaye responded that Rimbaud was no longer writing poetry,
and didn't even seem to remember ever having done so.

On 18 December Rimbaud's younger sister Vitalie succumbed
to a tuberculous synovitis at the age of seventeen. On the day of the
funeral, attendants were surprised to see that her brother – who

attributed to himself the vocation of 'professeur' for his appearance on her death certificate – had shaved his head as a sign of mourning.

The next few years would mark a period of furtive movement for the man Verlaine later referred to as 'l'homme aux semelles de vent' (the man with soles of wind). In the first weeks of 1876 he studied Russian from an old Greek–Russian dictionary. In the spring he went to Vienna, with his sights set on finding work in Russia. Upon his arrival in Vienna, however, he was beaten and robbed by a cab driver, and without coat, hat or money he was brought to the border by police, to return on foot to Charleville.[2] He then made his way from there through Brussels and Rotterdam to Harderwijk, where he enlisted for a six-year stint as a mercenary fighting in what was then known as the Dutch East Indies. In June his unit shipped off from DenHelder aboard the *Prins van Oranje*. When it arrived in Java in July, Rimbaud once again preferred not to fight; the authorities labelled him a deserter, so he kept a low profile for two weeks in Semarang, living off the three hundred florins he had received for enlisting. Two weeks later and under an assumed name, he was aboard a Scottish boat called the *Wandering Chief*. After passing through a vicious storm near the Cape of Good Hope, the *Wandering Chief* pulled into port in Queenstown, Ireland, in December. Rimbaud then possibly made his way to Paris – perhaps meeting up with Nouveau, who was thinking of Sinbad when he dubbed his friend 'Rimbald the Sailor' – and eventually back to Charleville yet again.

After the winter in Charleville, Rimbaud set out yet again, this time to the northeast. In early May he was in Cologne, speaking with a recruiting officer for the Dutch army. A week later, he wrote to the American consul in Bremen:

Bremen the 14 may 77
The untersigned [*sic*] Arthur Rimbaud – Born in Charleville (France) – Aged 23 – 5 ft. 6 height – Good healthy [*sic*], – Late

a teacher of sciences and languages – Recently deserted from
the 47° Regiment of the French army, – Actually in Bremen
without any means, the French Consul refusing any Relief, –

Would like to know on which conditions he could conclude
an immediate engagement in the American navy.

Speaks and writes English, German, French, Italian and
Spanish.

Has been four months as a sailor in a Scotch bark, from Java
to Queenstown, from August to December 76.

Would be very honoured and grateful to receive an answer.
John Arthur Rimbaud (*oc*, 466)

Without a positive reply, he kept moving, and he spent the summer
months working his way through the Nordic countries in jobs that
are as varied as they are unsubstantiated: according to Delahaye
he was an interpreter for the Loisset circus in Stockholm and
Copenhagen; the poet's sister Isabelle disputed the circus job and
claimed that he worked in a sawmill instead; and in June his name
appeared twice in a registry of foreigners in Stockholm, working first
in sales and then as a sailor. Either way, he was back in Charleville
in September, only to leave for Marseille, from there to sail to
Alexandria. But once again Marseille coincided with bad health, for
soon after setting sail he was taken with stomach pain so severe that
he disembarked at Civitavecchia. After a month of recuperation in
Rome he was back in Charleville, where he spent the better part of
the next year, with an alleged brief visit to Paris around Easter. The
farmers working his family's land had declined to renew their lease,
so Arthur helped his family – and his brother Frédéric, recently
returned from five years of military service – by working on the
farm. Unbeknown to him, in London the *Gentleman's Magazine*
published his poem 'Les Effarés' under the title 'Petits pauvres'
(Little Poor Ones); his past life as a poet was an increasingly
distant memory.

Paul Verlaine, sketch of Arthur Rimbaud, letter to Ernest Delahaye, March 1876.

On his 24th birthday he set off again, through Switzerland, again crossing the Gotthard pass on foot – but this time, in late October, through almost 1 metre (2 ft) of snow. He arrived in Milan and then went to Genoa, again planning to take a boat to Alexandria. Several letters from his family were waiting for him upon his arrival in Genoa, so he wrote a long response describing his trip and upcoming plans. The account of the gruelling crossing is far more impressive for the harrowing conditions that Rimbaud endured than for any particular literary flair to the writing: he devoted all his energies to getting through a blinding snowstorm that produced drifts up to his ribs as he climbed almost 5,000 metres (3 mi.) in elevation. The exploit of crossing the Gotthard Pass in such conditions was no less impressive for the insight it provides into the kind of traveller Rimbaud had become.[3] The transition from his early walking through the Ardennes countryside was nearly complete: leisurely, aimless wandering was replaced by perseverance towards a specific geographic destination, just as the writing to describe it left behind poetry and transcendence in favour of adventure and detailed description of the external world. Writing had become something else.

As he sat down on 17 November to describe the Gotthard Pass to his family, he had no way of knowing that his father had died the very same day in Dijon.

Two days later he set off for Alexandria, only to resurface in mid-December in Cyprus, where he was a quarry master in Larnaca. Six months later, having contracted typhoid fever, he left; Roche was yet again the site of convalescence, the calm pace of the methodical farm-work no doubt a welcome respite after the frenetic travelling. When Delahaye came for a visit he asked his old friend if he still thought about literature; bemused, Rimbaud said that he no longer bothered with such things. For Delahaye the proof that Rimbaud had truly changed was in how he found the winter harder and harder to bear. The days of wandering for days through rain and snow were behind him; he needed warmth, and spoke of living at least as far south as the Mediterranean. Rimbaud had amply shown that you could take the boy out of Charleville; perhaps you could take a bit of Charleville out of the boy, too. It would be the last time that the two friends would see each other.

Back in Cyprus in March 1880, Rimbaud was the 'clerk of works employed in Superintendence', earning £200 per month to oversee the construction site for the first permanent structure on Mount Troodos: the British governor's summer residence. The plaque that would later be affixed to the door – 'Arthur Rimbaud, French poet and genius, despite his fame contributed with his own hands to the construction of this house, 1881' (*IJL*, 779) – could hardly be more inaccurate. The date was wrong, while in Cyprus Rimbaud had no fame to disdain, and he didn't build anything with his hands (he most likely oversaw the construction of the workers' wooden lodgings, starting in May, and then the governor's palace's foundation). He left the worksite long before the project's completion, heading to Alexandria in June. The question of why he left before the job was finished is also ridden with doubt. He wrote to his mother that it was due to a financial dispute with his employers. To his employer in Aden he would later say that the Cyprus-based company went out of business. According to a later account by Ottorino Rosa, who accompanied Rimbaud in his exploration of Galla, Rimbaud confided in him a different reason: after throwing a rock that accidentally struck a worker in the head and killed him, Rimbaud fled and hid aboard a ship until it set sail.

After only two days in Alexandria he boarded a ship for the Red Sea, and in early August it pulled into Aden: specifically, into Tawahi, known as Steamer Point when Aden was a British Crown Colony city within the larger Aden Settlement. Situated on the southwest corner of the Arabian Peninsula, Aden enjoyed a great strategic position for commerce, since steamships would stop there on their way from the Mediterranean to the Indian Ocean. Despite falling ill upon his arrival in Aden, Rimbaud brought a recommendation from a Frenchman he had met en route and gave it to another compatriot, M. Dubar, who was working for the import–export trading company Viannay, Bardey & Company. Dubar hired him to oversee the workshop in which coffee beans were sorted before being put into bags, weighed and loaded onto ships bound for Marseille; he received 7 francs per day. In his new environs, Rimbaud was not entirely miserable; whereas the rest of Aden was insufferably hot in August, Steamer Point's cool breezes made it the preferred destination for many of the local Europeans, who enjoyed the Grand Hôtel de l'Univers and the Hôtel de l'Europe, both run by Frenchmen.

Rimbaud's boss Alfred Bardey was also moving quickly: having just founded the company in May, he had been in eastern Ethiopia setting up a new outpost in the walled city of Harar when the former poet arrived in Aden. By the time Bardey returned from his month away, Dubar was sufficiently impressed with Rimbaud, who by that time spoke Arabic so well that he was able to give orders to local workers. Upon learning that Bardey had put the Harar office in the hands of a D. Pinchard, Rimbaud asked to be sent to join him, and Bardey assented. On 10 November Rimbaud signed a three-year contract with the company for 1,800 rupees – the equivalent of 300 francs per month – as well as 1 per cent of the net profits from the Harar outfit. Heading to his new post, Rimbaud travelled from the Arabian Peninsula to Abyssinia with his new co-worker Constantin Righas; they crossed from Steamer Point to Zeila, a small port in present-day Somalia on the gulf that was then called Tadjoura, today Djibouti. If many of the cities along the eastern coast were economically depressed, Zeila was not: its thriving commercial activity included ivory, wheat, honey, gold and slaves (the French would nominally abolish the slave trade in Tadjoura in October 1889). After twenty days on horseback through the Somali desert, Righas and Rimbaud made it to Harar, the hilltop city at the time under Egyptian colonial occupation. Rimbaud wrote to his family that there were good opportunities to make money there, thanks to the healthy trade that included imported European goods brought to the city on camelback. Things were looking up. And then, a few weeks into his first stay in Harar, he fell ill again; it was syphilis, according to Bardey, who had gone to visit the company's new offices and helped his employee regain his strength with the aid of the medical facilities in the Egyptian garrison. (In March it would be Pinchard's turn: malarial fevers forced him to leave Harar for good.) Rimbaud's honeymoon period in Harar was brief, and he soon mentioned wanting to leave the city. In May he set out with his employee Constantin Sotiro to explore the Boubassa region and acquire goods for resale in Harar. Once back, he arranged for his profits to be sent back to his family in France and made plans to go back out for new expeditions – longer, and more dangerous – that would take him through the summer. September marked the beginning of the rainy season and the end of his stay in a city that he could no longer bear. He submitted his resignation to Bardey, who invited him back to the home office in Aden. He would spend 1882 there, only to return to Harar in March 1883.

Part of the Rimbaud myth has traditionally held that when he left Europe, he left writing behind. Although he no longer wrote poetry, the philomath's thirst for learning was never fully quenched, and so his sustained quest for otherness, in all its forms, took hold in new forms of experience and learning. In addition to the languages that he acquired, his turn towards the manual labour of docks and quarries was the practical side of the quest for scientific knowledge to which he had already alluded in some of the *Illuminations*, and when he discussed his baccalauréat with Delahaye. Reading and writing hardly disappeared, but rather underwent a series of substitutions.

In January 1881 he wrote to his family and asked them to forward
to a bookseller his request for

> a work by a German or Swiss writer, published in Germany
> a few years ago and translated into French, entitled *Guide du
> Voyageur* or *Manuel théorique et pratique de l'Explorateur*. (That's
> the title, more or less.) I have heard that the publication is a very
> intelligent compendium of all of the knowledge necessary to
> the explorer, in topography, mineralogy, hydrography, natural
> history, etc. etc. (*oc*, 486–7)

He also enclosed a letter for M. Bautin, an instrument maker
in Paris, declaring, 'I would like to know everything about the
best instruments in France (or abroad) for mathematics, optics,
astronomy, meteorology, pneumatics, mechanics, hydraulics and
mineralogy. I'm not interested in surgical instruments' (*oc*, 487).
A year later, he wrote to his family from Aden and asked them
to forward to Delahaye a letter in which he asks his old friend
to purchase some equipment, preferably 'with the assistance of
someone with expertise, for example a professor of mathematics
you might know': a travel theodolite, a sextant, a mineralogical
kit with three hundred samples, a pocket barometer, a surveyor's
line and a full mathematics set (*oc*, 505). He also asked Delahaye
for many more books, and the titles that he requested – and that
he read, according to the accounts of those who worked with him
– suggest a similar desire for scientific erudition: *Topographie et
géodésie*; *Trigonométrie*; *Minéralogie*; *Hydrographie*; *Météorologie*;
Chimie industrielle; *Manuel du voyageur*; *Instructions pour les voyageurs
préparateurs*; *Le Ciel* and, last but not least, *L'Annuaire du Bureau des
longitudes pour 1882*.

Rimbaud had never been one to accumulate books for the sake of
lining walls with impressive leather-bound tomes. The 'prodigieux
linguiste' was now immersing himself in the language of the world's

elements: writing was topography and hydrography, the *logos* was mineralogy and meteorology. Gone was the poetic vision that depended on the 'long, immense et raisonné dérèglement de *tous les sens*'; what had been immense – from the Latin *immensus*, immeasurable – was replaced with all that *could* be measured, be it in trigonometric angles or in all the shapes and sizes into which geodesy divides the world. This step is well beyond the shift in literary perspective from 'subjective' to 'objective', and Rimbaud's idea of scientific observation was beyond what poetry could contain. It might lack the poetic, but the measurable world was still worth contemplating, describing, even detailing. As he explained to his family and Delahaye in those letters from January 1882, he intended to write a study on Harar and the Gallas – the regions he had explored – and have it published. This study would indeed find its way into print: Rimbaud sent the 'Notice sur l'Ogadine', dated 10 December 1883, to Bardey, who sent it the following month to the Société de géographie de Paris; it was presented during its meeting of 1 February 1884 and included in the society's annual bulletin for 1884.

Remarkable for its description of parts of Abyssinia that had not previously been visited by European explorers, the writing itself is far from literary, but it is still writing, and it is helpful to think of Rimbaud less as turning his back on writing than as moving away from poetry to consider other worlds to explore, and other means to express them. After all, the project of the 'Voyant' proposed infusing the written text with what was *seen* – on some level at least – and Rimbaud's creative impulses remained true to this combination in Africa: a flat, unliterary writing married to a more creative visual component. As he explained in the same letters from January 1882, he was waiting to receive photographic equipment that he had sent for, from Lyon; he said that it would be very profitable and that his geographic study would include his own photographs as illustrations. Such a combination of text and image was not new to Rimbaud: a decade earlier, illustrations and texts of all sorts had crowded the pages of the *Album zutique*, and before that Rimbaud had mentioned to Delahaye the idea of a series of prose poems to be entitled *Photographie des temps passés*, no doubt inspired by the new industry that rose from the ruins of the Paris Commune. But the Commune was also when Rimbaud still believed in poetic language and its ability to reveal an *other* world by 'voyance'. A decade later, the former poet in Africa could compensate for his loss of confidence in poetic language with a turn to photography – to images of a world that was to his eyes literally, exotically, 'other'. As Rimbaud drew inspiration from his scientific readings and imagined the works in which he would transcribe his observations, the more he felt that photography had a role to play, with promising results. At least, such is how Rimbaud described them to his family, as each time he mentions them in the spring and summer of 1883 he calls them 'curious':

Besides, I am planning on making a curious album of photographs (19 March 1883; *oc*, 524)

Everyone wants to be photographed here, they even offer a guinea per photo. I haven't yet gotten settled, nor in the know of what's going on; but I will do so quickly, and I will send you curious things. (6 May 1883; *oc*, 526).

I received the letter in which you acknowledge receipt of the photographs. Thank you. Those ones were not very interesting; I had given up on that series because of the rain, the sun not having appeared for three months. I will take it up again when good weather comes and I could send you some truly curious things (26 August 1883; *oc*, 533)

Today the Musée Rimbaud possesses all but one of the photographs taken by Rimbaud the photographer, which include a view of the

Arthur Rimbaud, a *daboula* maker during khât time, Harar, 1883.

Arthur Rimbaud, self-portrait in a banana grove, Harar, 1883.

market in Harar, one of the mausoleum of Cheikh-Ubader, patron
saint of Harar, a portrait taken at khât time of a worker making
daboula (goat skins used for storing coffee beans), and a portrait
of Sotiro.[4] Three other photos from Harar in 1883 survive: three
self-portraits. If Rimbaud considered them curious, it could be at
least in part because the French word *autoportrait* would not exist
for another 45 years; in his letter to his mother on 6 May he enclosed
what he called 'photographies de moi-même par moi-même' (*oc*,
526). Whether standing in front of a banana tree or on a terrace,
the tanned former poet's facial expression is hard to make out.[5]

A few fuzzy photographs and bits of hearsay fill in some gaps of
what remains an incomplete portrait of *Rimbaud l'africain*. Group
photographs include one taken in 1883 near Aden commemorating
a hunting expedition (Rimbaud is standing, his left arm crossed in
front of his chest) and an August 1880 photo of Europeans posing
on the balcony of Aden's Hôtel de l'Univers; the man seated second
from the right was said to be Rimbaud when the photograph was

The balcony of the Hôtel de l'Univers, Aden, 1880; Rimbaud is believed to be the
young man seated second from right.

At Sheikh Othman in Aden, *c.* 1883.

presented to the public in April 2010. As tantalizing as it would
be to have such a clear image of Rimbaud in his adult days, the
debate that raged in the French press – going so far as to include
biometric analysis – left varying degrees of certitude as to whether
the man in that photograph was really Rimbaud. Fortunately
his poetry left a more convincing impression, and even more
enthusiasm.

For at the same time Rimbaud was appearing elsewhere, in
print. In 1882 Félicien Champsaur published *Dinah Samuel*, a
roman-à-clef that included a number of profiles of the Parisian
literary scene, with which Champsaur was very familiar. In one
chapter, an Impressionist painter tries to convince a writer that
a certain Arthur Cimber – whose name would appear as 'Arthur
Rimbaud' in the novel's second edition (1886) – is the greatest poet
on earth, with two stanzas of 'Les Chercheuses de poux' offered as
justification of the title. The following year, while Rimbaud was
on the expedition to the Ogadine region that would lead to the

account published by the Société de géographie de Paris, his name was already in the papers: in the October and November issues of the journal *Lutèce*, Verlaine published a description of his former partner in his series entitled *Les Poètes maudits* (Damned Poets).[6] In more than three times the number of words he had used in his opening essay on Tristan Corbière, Verlaine meticulously presented this precocious and unique poetic talent to a public that, for the most part, had not heard much of him, if at all. His long-lost friend receives the most sympathetic of introductions:

> We had the joy of knowing Monsieur Arthur Rimbaud. Today various things separate us from him but, of course, our very deep admiration for his genius has never wavered.
>
> At the relatively distant time when we knew him, Monsieur Arthur Rimbaud was a child of sixteen and seventeen years old, already endowed with all the poetic baggage that he would need, as the public knew and as we will attempt to analyse while quoting as much as we can.
>
> The man was tall, well built, almost athletic, with the perfectly oval face of an angel in exile, with light-brown tousled hair and blue eyes with a disturbing pale hue. From the Ardennes, he possessed, in addition to a regional accent that he lost too quickly, the gift of quick assimilation that is common to people from that region, – which could explain the rapid drying out, under the savage Paris sun, of his style, to borrow a phrase from our forefathers whose direct and correct language wasn't always incorrect, in fact! (*OPC*, 643–4)

Verlaine includes a number of poems in their entirety, and thus presents a veritable anthology to readers of *Lutèce*: 'Voyelles', 'Oraison du soir', 'Les Assis', 'Les Effarés', 'Les Chercheuses de poux' and 'Le Bateau ivre' appear *in extenso*, followed by extracts from 'Les Premières Communions' and 'L'Orgie parisienne ou Paris se

Cover of Paul Verlaine, *Les Poètes maudits* (1886).

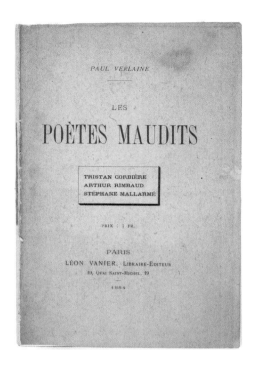

PAUL VERLAINE

LES

POÈTES MAUDITS

TRISTAN CORBIÈRE
ARTHUR RIMBAUD
STÉPHANE MALLARMÉ

PRIX : 3 FR.

PARIS
LÉON VANIER, Libraire-Éditeur
19, Quai Saint-Michel, 19

1884

repeuple', and references to a number of other poems, including 'Les Accroupissements', 'Les Pauvres à l'Église', 'Les Douaniers', 'Les Mains de Jeanne-Marie', 'Les Sœurs de Charité' and 'L'Éternité'. The most amazing poem of all, Verlaine says, is 'Les Veilleurs' (The Vigils):

> the 'Vigils', a poem which is – alas! – no longer in our possession, and which our memory would not be able to reconstitute, left the strongest impression that verses ever caused us to feel. It is of a vibration, of a breadth, of a sacred sadness! And of such an accent of sublime desolation, that we dare say that of what Monsieur Arthur Rimbaud wrote it is the most beautiful, by far!
> (*OPC*, 654)

Unfortunately, this poem has not been found; it remains the one that got away.

The two disconnected, parallel worlds would press on: the capitalist explorer constantly on the move in Africa and, in France, growing appreciation for his former literary life. Bardey's Harar office closed in March 1884, and so in June Rimbaud signed a new contract with its successor, Bardey frères, to work in Aden; the city would be his home for the next sixteen months. In France, a new generation of poets was inspired by the poetry they discovered in Verlaine's essay, particularly 'Voyelles'; they would soon assemble under the banner of the Symbolist movement and anoint Rimbaud one of their precursors. In May 1885, some two million Parisians filed through the city streets to pay their final respects to Victor Hugo after his death; the world of French poetry had lost one of its giants. Far away in Africa, the former *poète maudit* was considering less poetic pursuits; in October, sensing that he could make more money elsewhere instead of overseeing a lazy coffee trade, he left Bardey's company for a new adventure. He might have been afraid of 'la mitraille' when it belonged to the Carlists, but he was not afraid now; he decided to lead a caravan and deliver guns to Menelik II, King of the Shewa region, who was at war against Emperor Jean of Abyssinia. (Back in Paris, Camille Mauclair and Gabriel Vicaire were preparing their parody of Rimbaud's poem 'Oraison du soir', to appear in their novel *Les Délinquescences d'André Floupette* in 1885.) The former poet explained to his mother that he would sell Menelik 2,000 rifles that had been declared unfit for use: purchased for 7 or 8 francs each, he planned on selling them for forty apiece. To deliver them to Menelik he had to cross the Red Sea, and from Tadjoura his caravan had to get through hundreds of miles of uncharted desert territories that were inhospitable because of their natural wasteland and the bandits who roamed there. He finally set off in October 1886, a few months and a few thousand miles away from growing literary recognition in Paris.

The contrast between his growing literary success and his failed commercial sale to Menelik could hardly have been starker. Rimbaud's two business partners died, and he was the victim of theft. In February 1887 he made it to Ankober, the capital of Shewa region, but Menelik was off fighting 190 kilometres (120 mi.) away in Entoto (now Addis Ababa), so his caravan had further to go to close the deal. When he finally arrived there two months later, Rimbaud discovered that Menelik was no longer willing to pay the price they had agreed on. Downtrodden, he returned to Harar with the explorer Jules Borelli to receive some modest payment from the provincial governor Ras Makonnen. If only Rimbaud had been in Paris in May and July 1886 instead of planning his sale to Menelik; *La Vogue* published poems from *Illuminations* in five successive issues. The first publications of French free-verse poetry included Rimbaud's 'Marine' in the 29 May issue and 'Mouvement' on 21 June.[7] All two hundred copies of the first printing of the standalone volume of *Illuminations* – which erroneously included some verse poems from 1872 – would appear that autumn with a preface by Verlaine; it was in this preface that Verlaine offered the subtitle that he said Rimbaud had intended, 'Coloured Plates'.

[the volume] is composed of short pieces, exquisite prose or deliciously and expressly false verses. There is no overarching idea, or at least we can't find one. The obvious joy of being a great poet, such fairylike landscapes, adorable vague loves sketched out and the highest ambition (achieved) of style: such is the résumé that we think we can dare give the following work. It is up to the reader to admire it in detail. [. . .]

He has been declared dead several times. We are unaware of this detail, which would make us quite sad. May he know it, in case it is not true. For we were once his friend, and remain so from afar. (*opc*, 631–2)

Despite having been declared dead, Rimbaud was still alive, although not by much. By July 1887 he was back in Aden and exhausted: weary from travelling, in need of some rest – during which, of course, he would continue to write. Cairo offered some respite in August, and that month *Le Bosphore égyptien* published his account of the expedition through Shewa. Rimbaud was not alone in Aden; his servant Djami Wadaï was with him. Little is known about Djami other than that he was originally from Harar, he was married and he had a child. Djami had been with Rimbaud since 1884 and would remain with him until Rimbaud's death. Djami was so important to him that Rimbaud called for him on his deathbed; in his one and only bequest he left him 750 thalers (3,000 francs). He was not the only person in the inner circle during Rimbaud's life in Africa, however; witnesses who knew him in Aden say that in 1883 or 1884 he lived with an Abyssinian woman who was very sweet, tall and slender, and rather pretty. About her, too, all that is known comes through unsubstantiated claims, although a letter from August 1884 mentions Rimbaud travelling with a woman called Mariam. Given his propensity for acquiring languages it is not impossible that he taught her to read and speak French, and apparently she wore European clothing and smoked cigarettes, and Bardey's housekeeper Françoise Grisard taught her how to sew. This relationship, which Bardey described as intimate, was as close as Rimbaud would come to having a family of his own, as he had mused in the letter to his mother and siblings that accompanied his self-portraits:

> I regret having never gotten married or had a family. But for now I'm condemned to wander, attached to a faraway business, and every day I lose the taste for the climate, the way of life, and even the language of Europe. Alas! What's the point of all these comings and goings, this exhaustion, these adventures with people of strange races, these languages that fill up my memory, and these nameless difficulties if someday, after several years,

'Mariam', Rimbaud's companion in Aden, early 1880s.

I can't rest in a more or less pleasing spot, and find a family, and have at least a son that I spend the rest of my life raising as it suits me, decorating and arming him with the most complete knowledge attainable at the time, and watching him become a renowned engineer, a man made powerful and rich by science? But who knows how many days I will last in these mountains? And I could disappear in the midst of these peoples without news of it ever getting out. (*oc*, 527)

The relationship with the Abyssinian woman lasted no more than two years, and Bardey said that Rimbaud had sent her back home with some money when he left Bardey's company – that is, when he set off to cut his deal with Menelik.

Fully rested, Rimbaud returned to Aden, hatching new plans about building an arms factory in Shewa and running guns for his fellow Frenchman Armand Savouré. As Savouré explained of the month he stayed with Rimbaud in Harar in the autumn of 1888, writing was still a central, regular activity: Savouré never once learned where Rimbaud slept, since he would sit at his desk, writing day and night.[8] Perhaps Rimbaud had finally learned his lesson about guns; he joined forces with merchant César Tian and opened a trading post in Harar, leading a quiet if boring existence buying, selling and bartering whatever he could get his hands on. During this period, he befriended the Swiss engineer Alfred Ilg, who would become Menelik's prime minister after the latter drove out the Egyptians and was crowned Emperor. It was Ilg who on 23 August 1890 wrote to Rimbaud discouraging the purchasing of slaves. Since Ilg wrote that he recognized Rimbaud's good intentions, and without evidence or eyewitness accounts of Rimbaud's doing anything else, it seems most likely that the former poet inquired about the feasibility of trading slaves without ever engaging in it. He focused his energies on buying and selling anything else, but not people.

He certainly had time and the opportunity to re-engage with his writerly past if he wanted to, but he didn't. After Rimbaud offered some pieces on his African expeditions to his former classmate Paul Bourde, who was writing for *Le Temps*, in late February 1888 Bourde wrote back indicating his interest in such texts and adding some thoughts on an altogether different topic:

> You probably don't know, living so far from us, that you have become, in a little cenacle, a sort of legendary figure: one of these notables who are thought to be dead, but in whose existence some faithful enthusiasts continue to believe, and for whose return they obstinately await. Your first poems, in prose and in verse, were published in some journals in the Latin Quarter and even collected in a volume. Some young people (whom I personally find naive) tried to base a literary system on your sonnet about the colour of letters. This little group, who claim you as their master despite not knowing what has become of you, hope you will one day reappear to rescue them from obscurity. (*oc*, 641–2)

It is not known if Rimbaud responded to Bourde, but he cherished the letter enough to keep it. Two years later he received a similarly flattering letter, this time from Laurent de Gavoty, editor of the Marseille-based journal *La France moderne*:

> Monsieur and dear poet,
>   I have read your beautiful poems: this explains how happy and proud I would be to see the head of the Decadent and Symbolist School contribute to *La France moderne*. Please join us. (*oc*, 746)

To this letter a reply is also unknown, but somehow the journal learned that it had reached its destination, for in its issue of

19 February 1891 the journal announced its news proudly on the top of its third page:

> This time we've got him!
>
> We know where Arthur Rimbaud is, the great Arthur Rimbaud, the real Arthur Rimbaud, the Rimbaud of the *Illuminations*.
>
> This is not a decadent joke. We affirm that we know the den of the famous missing person.

If Rimbaud was swayed by either of these invitations, he did not let anyone know. The writer who had referred to earlier literary attempts as follies *while he was still writing poetry* was not about to turn back now. His previous life as a poet was the furthest thing from his mind; Bardey was shocked when Bourde later told him that the young man in his employ had been a talented poet, and the precious few times it came up Rimbaud was uneasy about what he allegedly called 'dregs' from a time in his life that he looked on as a period of general *ivresse*, in both its literal and its figurative meanings.

Another reason that Gavoty and readers of his *France moderne* would not hear more is that 'the great Arthur Rimbaud, the real Arthur Rimbaud' was in pain: great pain, real pain. The sad coincidence is that the same month that the journal announced it had tracked him down, Rimbaud was slowed considerably: his right knee was so painful that 'l'homme aux semelles de vent' had trouble walking. At first he assumed that it was arthritis, but the pain became so great that he had to close up shop, and he had a canvas cot constructed so that he could be carried over 240 kilometres (150 mi.) of desert to Zeila. The journey was not easy: crossing the desert took eleven days, and the boat to Aden took an additional three. The European doctor who saw Rimbaud in Zeila diagnosed tubercular synovitis – common in rheumatoid arthritis – and recommended amputation. Weakened and undernourished

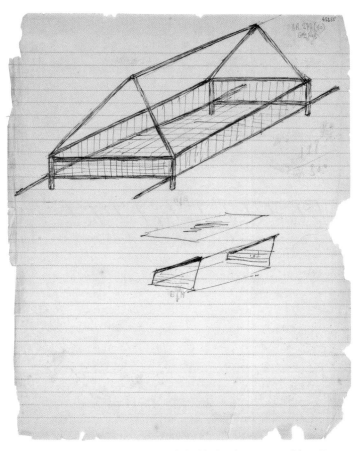

Arthur Rimbaud, sketch of the stretcher he had built to be transported from Harar to Zeilah.

as he was, Rimbaud's condition did not improve after two weeks in hospital, and doctors encouraged him to return to France to be treated. Again, travel: thirteen days from Aden to Marseille, where he arrived on 20 May and was immediately admitted to the Hôpital de la Conception. Two days later, telegrams flew between Marseille and Roche (*oc*, 773):

MADAME RIMBAUD, ROCHES
NEAR ATTIGNY
ARDENNES
TODAY YOU OR ISABELLE COME MARSEILLE BY EXPRESS
TRAIN MONDAY MORNING THEY WILL AMPUTATE MY LEG
DANGER DEATH SERIOUS AFFAIRS TO SETTLE ARTHUR HÔPITAL
CONCEPTION RESPOND —RIMBAUD.

The response was swift (this was not a time to be wordy):

ARTHUR RIMBAUD, HÔPITAL
CONCEPTION, MARSEILLE
I AM LEAVING NOW WILL BE THERE TOMORROW NIGHT COURAGE
AND PATIENCE —W^{IDOW} RIMBAUD.

The operation to amputate above his knee was a success, and 'la Mother' was waiting for him when he arrived in his recovery room. The procedure revealed that the pain was caused not by synovitis but by osteosarcoma. Ever the nurturer, Mme Rimbaud returned to the Ardennes after she saw him in recovery.

As soon as he could, Rimbaud tried to keep moving: first with crutches, then with a wooden prosthesis. The irony of this reduced mobility was not lost on him:

So I'm starting to walk again, with crutches. What a nuisance, how tiring and how sad when I think about my old travels, and

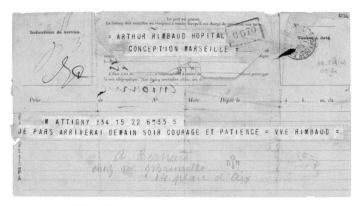

Telegram from Widow Rimbaud to her son, 22 May 1891.

how I was active just five months ago! Where are the trips across mountains, cavalcades, strolls, deserts, rivers and seas? And now, I'm a one-legged *cripple*. I'm starting to understand that crutches, wooden legs and mechanical legs are a bunch of jokes and with all that you end up dragging yourself around miserably without ever being able to do anything. And I who had just decided to return to France this summer to get married! Goodbye marriage, goodbye family, goodbye future! My life is over, I'm nothing more than an immobile stump [. . .] (*oc*, 785)

Two weeks later he would be moving again: by means of a special train car he made it back up to Roche, where he hadn't been in a decade. His sister Isabelle cared for him, and after a month she accompanied him back to Marseille. There he hoped that his condition could be treated better and that, once he improved, he could easily get back to Africa. But the cancer had spread, and he quickly got worse. He called for Djami and asked to travel again, this time to return to Harar; no such journey would occur.

The record of Rimbaud's last weeks comes to us from Isabelle's journal and letters. Despite her posthumous whitewashing of many

Isabelle Rimbaud, undated.

aspects of her brother's life and work, her accounts of her brother's physical condition in his final weeks seem reliable. As she wrote to her mother on 28 October,

> Death is approaching fast. I told you in my last letter, my dear mother, that his stump was extremely swollen. Now there is an enormous cancerous growth between his hip and his belly, just on top of the bone. His stump, which was so sensitive and painful, has almost stopped making him suffer. Arthur hasn't seen the deadly tumour: he's surprised that everyone keeps coming to see the poor stump where he no longer feels anything; and all the doctors (at least ten have been in to see him) are speechless and terrified by this strange cancer.
>
> For now, it's his poor head and left arm that hurt him most. But he is most often in a deep lethargy, apparently asleep, during which he hears all the sounds with a singular clarity. He gets a shot of morphine to help him sleep.
>
> When he wakes, he brings his life to an end by a sort of continuous dream: he says strange things very sweetly, in a voice that would enchant me if it weren't breaking my heart.
>
> [. . .]
>
> In fact the doctors have basically stopped checking in, because he cries so much while talking to them and it upsets them so. He recognizes everyone. He sometimes calls me Djami [. . .] we are in Harar, we are still leaving for Aden, and we have to get the camels and organize the caravan; he is walking very easily with his new prosthetic leg, we go for a few long rides on richly saddled mules; then we have to work, keep the books, write letters. Quickly, quickly, they're waiting for us, we have to close our suitcases and leave. [. . .] And then he starts crying [. . .]
>
> He no longer eats much of anything, and what little he does take he does with extreme repugnance. As a result he's as thin

as a skeleton and as pale as a cadaver. And all of his poor limbs paralysed, mutilated, dead all around him! Oh God, what a pity![9]

During his final weeks Rimbaud was in and out of a coma, in and out of delirium; and if Isabelle's description of her brother's physical state is reliable, her pious nature and his own long-held anticlerical ideas are enough to doubt the religious confession that she claimed took place, as she reported it in letters to her mother and as it informed posthumous publications. In her hand, however, we have Rimbaud's last letter, which he dictated to her. To the director of the Messageries Maritimes shipping company he provides an inventory of five lots containing twelve tusks and requests that he change to a service of something called 'Aphinar', which can lead him to Suez. Still hatching future plans.

> All the services there are everywhere, and I, infirm, miserable, I cannot find anything, the first dog in the street will tell you so.
> Please send me the price for services from Aphinar to Suez. I am completely paralysed. I would therefore like to be on board well in advance. Tell me at what time I should be carried aboard. (*oc*, 803)

He was either unaware of or unwilling to accept the idea that he was in no condition to travel.

Nor was he aware of the storm swirling around his poetry back in Paris. The author Rodolphe Darzens – who had purchased the *recueil Demeny* – had undertaken a biographical study of Rimbaud that would include unpublished poems. Despite initially agreeing to publish it, the editor Léon Genonceaux was more interested in the poems; they would make a fine volume, with Darzen's essay relegated to a preface. Genonceaux took the rough notes and poems that Darzens had shown him for what was to be called *Sur Arthur*

Arthur Rimbaud, a few days before his death.

Plaque on the old Hôpital de la Conception, Marseille.

Rimbaud and baptized it *Reliquaire* (an old title from François Coppée, who had given his permission). Without Darzens seeing page proofs or giving his approval, Genonceaux published 550 copies of *Reliquaire*, bringing nineteen previously unpublished poems to the public. When he learned of it, Darzens filed a complaint, and police seized the 119 copies that were still in the editor's possession.

Isabelle dutifully wrote her brother's dictated letter in Marseille's Hôpital de la Conception on 9 November 1891. The Paris police took possession of *Reliquaire* that same day, at 5 p.m. As writing and travel were reduced to a dictated letter and a dream, poetry was being pulled back from the public.

At ten o'clock the following morning, Arthur Rimbaud left this world, at the age of 37.

7

Afterlives

I think there are many Rimbauds in this world and that their number will increase in time.

Henry Miller[1]

When the abbot who was to oversee Rimbaud's burial in the Charleville family plot encouraged Mme Rimbaud to contact the deceased's former friends so that they could attend the funeral on 14 November, she curtly told him not to bother, that it wasn't worth it. Not even his brother Frédéric was there: only his mother and his sister, the smallest of fan clubs.

And yet, since his death, every generation has claimed Rimbaud. This practice took hold in the first years after he died – truth be told, it had even begun when he was merely presumed dead – and it continues to this day. The poet still receives so much correspondence that authorities installed a mailbox in the Charleville-Mézières cemetery where he finally stopped moving.

The unwavering enthusiasm for Rimbaud's life and work can be traced to a series of questions that, while they will always go unanswered, fascinate and tantalize us without frustrating us to the point of giving up. They can get long and wordy, but the short version is: Who was he? Necessary, related questions are: What can his poems tell us? What might they mean? A longer version goes something like: What kind of person could revolutionize an entire

Tomb of Arthur Rimbaud and his sister, Vitalie Rimbaud.

literary genre, only to turn his back on it by the age of 21 and pursue a life so different from the one he started with?

If these questions will forever prove elusive, it is in part because Rimbaud already answered them; we just refuse to be satisfied with his answers. His answers were insufficient from the moment he thought of them; that he chose to write them anyway shows the extent to which he continues to play with us. The understanding of Rimbaud explores and illustrates, with emphasis, the very problematics of reading: of texts, poetic and not; and of historical phenomena more generally. And yet the life and work are so compelling that we continue to read, prod and attempt to understand by returning to the most fundamental of questions, even though we have already heard the answers.

Who was he?

He already told us: 'Je est un autre.'

What can his poems tell us? What might they mean?

We already have his answers: 'J'ai seul la clef de cette parade sauvage,' and 'trouvez Hortense'.

So each generation has answered these questions in its own way, pinning down Rimbaud's life and times, unlocking the 'parade sauvage' and finding Hortense as they suited. Each generation has come up with answers, sure of itself, and each generation has been wrong. Or at least not entirely right. Biographers present the life they want to present, just as literary critics read how they want to read: favouring this or that part. Poems thought to have been lost forever magically resurface, as do previously unknown texts and photographs. Some of these missing puzzle pieces are legitimate, others are forgeries, and still others remain in dispute. They all keep alive the hope that more pieces will be brought forward to fill in the blanks. After all, Mathilde Mauté's claim of having destroyed all of the papers in her possession has not stood the test of time; the previously unknown early version of 'Mémoire' entitled 'd'Edgar Poe. Famille maudite' suddenly appeared in 2004 in the catalogue of an auction house that was selling papers that had been in Mathilde's possession. 'Le Rêve de Bismarck' only existed through some recollections from Delahaye before it was discovered in 2008. How many other scraps of paper in Ardennais attics contain unpublished texts signed 'Jean Baudry' or 'Arthur Rimbaud'? Where is 'Les Veilleurs', the poem that Verlaine said was Rimbaud's greatest? How many photographs from Aden or Harar in the 1880s include short-cropped moustachioed Europeans in their thirties, and how can we know if Rimbaud is among them?

Each generation has come up with its own answers to these questions. Of course, succeeding generations confront questions and answers about every author who has left a trace, every person who has left a trace. What makes Rimbaud exceptional in this regard is the degree to which – question after question, answer after answer – he remains unknown to us. And so each generation keeps coming up with its own answers to these questions.

Ernest Pignon-Ernest, portrait of Rimbaud, 1978.

Many of the early answers came from the hagiography of the poet's sister Isabelle, who was at his bedside when he died and who sketched her sibling's face in his final hours. In March 1897 Pierre Dufour – who had adopted the pseudonym Paterne Berrichon for his literary aspirations – contacted Mme Rimbaud to ask for her daughter's hand in marriage; although he had not seen Isabelle in person, he had been courting her via a steady correspondence over the previous eight months. Not knowing much about him, 'la Mother' contacted a number of his literary acquaintances for their approval. The fear of having another writer in the family was apparently not too great; the couple were married in 1897. Together they set out to present to an increasingly fervent public the Rimbaud that they wanted to present: respectable, of good moral character and traditional values. As they saw it, his relationship with Verlaine had been strictly between poems and not between the sheets, and on his death bed he rediscovered and accepted the Catholic faith that had been with him all along.

At the same time, the historians Jean Bourguignon and Charles Houin contributed a series of biographical articles to the *Revue d'Ardenne et d'Argonne*. Isabelle and Berrichon did not want the public to learn about the salacious details of Rimbaud's life; their subsequent attempts to present him in the best possible light led them to manipulate, withhold or falsify facts (altering wording in his poems, withholding or refuting biographical details and pieces of personal correspondence). Berrichon also established the divide between the poet and the man of action, publishing Rimbaud's poetic works separately (after jettisoning a third of the poems) from his letters from Africa and the Arabian Peninsula (from which two-thirds were excluded). While the suppressed texts have found their way into modern readers' hands, Berrichon's split between life and work has long influenced how we think of Rimbaud today.

Far more familiar with Rimbaud during the years of his poetic activity, Verlaine would return regularly to the study that he established in *Les Poètes maudits*: in the preface to *Illuminations* (1886); as part of the series *Hommes d'aujourd'hui* (1888); and in an article published in *La Revue indépendante* (1892). After watching rival journals publish Rimbaud (the *Poètes maudits* essay appeared in *Lutèce*, and poems from *Illuminations* in *La Vogue*), in 1886 and 1888 *Le Décadent* concocted a handful of poems that it claimed to be from the missing poet. Verlaine vigorously denounced the poor imitations; other fake Rimbauds were to come. Finally, Verlaine wrote the preface to the first major edition of Rimbaud's *Poésies complètes*, published by Léon Vanier in 1895, the year before Verlaine's death.

New editions meant that more than a handful of acquaintances were reading Rimbaud's work, and subsequent generations of writers marvelled at his artistry and the spark of his work that ignites, illuminates and explodes through the very raw materials that they shared. After the Symbolists, one of the early self-declared acolytes was fellow poet Paul Claudel, who was not merely inspired by Rimbaud's poetry; he claimed that reading Rimbaud's poems led directly to his recovering his lost faith. Claudel thus established the myth of the Christian Rimbaud, which he solidified in the preface that he contributed to Berrichon's 1912 edition of Rimbaud's complete works.[2]

The Claudel–Berrichon image of Rimbaud would hold sway until the next decade, when the Surrealists took charge of him. After claiming Rimbaud as one of their own in their first manifesto of 1924, the following year they addressed an open letter to Claudel – then the French ambassador to Japan – in which they wrestled the Charleville poet away from Claudel and the Church. For the Surrealists it was the unconscious, not the spiritual, that formed the foundation of Rimbaud's revolutionary poetics and transcendent world view. A decade later, André Breton famously ended a speech in June 1935 by comparing Rimbaud to Marx, saying that their very separate calls for different kinds of revolution were one and the same. The Surrealists also helped retrieve the bawdy, lewd and downright obscene elements of Rimbaud's work from censorship; in the preface to his *Anthologie de l'humour noir* (1940) André Breton called him a god of puberty.

Rimbaud's work also gained increased attention outside France, and his influence is evident in the work of writers as diverse as W. H. Auden, Stefan Zweig, Ezra Pound, Vladimir Nabokov and Jack Kerouac, among many others. One recurring theme has been to reflect on what it means to turn one's back on such obvious and exceptional literary talent. Marvelling at the move, René Char devoted a prose poem to it: 'Tu as bien fait de partir, Arthur Rimbaud!' (You did well to leave, Arthur Rimbaud!) from his collection *Fureur et Mystère* (1948). In his *L'Homme révolté* (1951), Albert Camus focussed less on the loss of literature than on the nature of the revolt against conventions, while Henry Miller felt that such a departure from the heights of poetry amounted to a doomsday act on a level with dropping an atomic bomb (*The Time of the Assassins*, 1956). As increased attention brings the alternative into the mainstream, it was inevitable that the unconventional would be canonized. Rimbaud's life and work drew so much attention that he became an automatic emblem for poetic rebellion. Not all of the attention would always be flattering, though; in sarcastic comments about a fictional scholar in Michel Houellebecq's *Submission* (2015), Rimbaud is derisively painted as the most boring thesis topic in universities around the world – or, to be precise, the second most boring, after Flaubert.

Each generation has had its edition of Rimbaud's work, as well. After Darzens and Verlaine, after Berrichon and Claudel, it was subjected to more shaping and redefining. Henry de Bouillane de Lacoste's careful philological analyses helped to elucidate a number of manuscripts with near-indecipherable handwriting and poems that were seemingly impossible to date with accuracy. His work, along with the entrance of Rimbaud's complete works in Gallimard's 'Bibliothèque de la Pléiade' series in 1946, would herald a move away from the psychological and political towards the historical and philological.[3]

On 19 May 1949 the philologists suddenly had their hands full. The journal *Combat* published extracts from 'La Chasse spirituelle' (The Spiritual Hunt), an apparently lost and unpublished poem by Rimbaud. With the scholar Pascal Pia attesting to the work's authenticity, Mercure de France published the text as a book. André Breton smelled a rat, and he was right: two actors, named Akakia Viala and Nicolas Bataille, soon admitted to having created the forgery as an act of revenge for the poor press that their theatrical adaptation of *Une saison en enfer* had received.[4] A few weeks later, the Pléiade editor Jules Mouquet announced the discovery of a different unpublished text by Rimbaud: entitled 'Lettre du Baron de Petdechèvre à son secrétaire au château de Saint-Magloire' and attributed to a certain Jean Marcel, it had been published on 16 September 1871 in the Charleville-based journal *Le Nord-est*, which claimed that it was a reprint of what had appeared in *Le Progrès* the previous week, on 9 September. Since Rimbaud had worked for *Le Progrès des Ardennes*, and without paper copies of the newspaper to support or deny any claims – in 1949 the discovery of 'Le Rêve de Bismarck' was still a long way off – Mouquet was convinced that no one else in Charleville was capable of writing such a text, and that 'Jean Marcel' was a pseudonym for Rimbaud. But it wasn't; *Le Progrès des Ardennes* had ceased activity in April 1871, and the *Progrès* in question was *Le Progrès de Lyon* (which, unlike its Ardennais cousin, actually did publish an issue on 9 September 1871).

Similar questions had surrounded the sonnet 'Poison perdu' (Lost Poison), published by Octave Mirbeau and attributed to an unknown poet in an issue of *Le Gaulois* from 1882. Verlaine

Graffiti in rue Pavée, Paris, 2010.

claimed that the poem he had recalled from memory was by
Rimbaud. Charles Morice expressed his doubts to Verlaine
immediately, and more questions were raised when the manuscript
was published in 1923: whose handwriting was it? Rimbaud's?
Forain's? Germain Nouveau had mentioned the sonnet in a letter
to Mallarmé in September 1874; it is most likely that the poem is
Nouveau's, although the degree of Rimbaud's influence is unknown.
To counter such vagaries – and especially after the 'La Chasse
spirituelle' and the 'Lettre du Baron de Petdechèvre' forgeries –
literary critics doubled down, insisting on an uncompromising
and exacting focus on the texts themselves: philological proof
for manuscripts, verifiable details in the biography. In January
1952 they found an ally in René Étiemble, who decided to set
the record straight when he defended his doctoral thesis on *le
mythe de Rimbaud*. Étiemble's exhaustive study of the reception

of Rimbaud's work pushed back hard against the misprision and misinterpretation that had run amok.

Other scholarly endeavours resonated beyond the academy, such as when Wallace Fowlie (completing his translation of Rimbaud's complete works) met with his colleague Henri Matarasso the day after Picasso had hastily sketched for Matarasso a copy of Étienne Carjat's famous portrait of Rimbaud. Fowlie was able to use the sketch for the cover of his translation, which drew the attention of Jim Morrison, lead singer of The Doors; Morrison wrote to Fowlie in 1968, saying that he carried the translation with him wherever he went. The inspiration for the song 'Wild Child' (from the album *The Soft Parade*, 1969, after being released the previous year as the B-side of 'Touch Me') comes more from Rimbaud's rebellious life than from whatever Morrison gleaned from the poems, however.

As Jim Morrison's interest suggests, Rimbaud was hardly a writer to be stashed away in dusty lecture halls, and when the university spilled out into the streets of Paris in May 1968, Rimbaud was on the front lines; if he wasn't on the barricades in 1871, he wouldn't miss his chance this time. While workers went on strike and brought factories to a standstill, French university students rejected stifling institutions that had not evolved since the end of the Second World War. Their utopian slogans included phrases from Rimbaud's poetry, including 'Il faut être absolument moderne' (We must be absolutely modern; from 'Adieu', *Une saison en enfer*) and, from 'Délires I: Vierge folle. L'Époux infernal' in *Une saison en enfer*:

'Changer la vie' (from 'Il a peut-être des secrets pour *changer la vie?*', or 'Does he have perhaps secrets for *changing life?*')[5]
'L'amour est à réinventer' (Love is to be reinvented)
'La vraie vie est absente' (Real life is absent)

The revolutionary aspirations of May '68 did not fully change French life, and instead were appropriated by the political apparatus when the French Socialist Party was resurrected in Épinay in 1971. The Party made 'Changer la vie' the title of its political programme in 1972 as well as of the hymn written for its June 1977 congress in Nantes, on the heels of municipal elections that had seen great gains on the left. The seeds of the students' slogans led to the institutionalization of anti-capitalism claims that would in turn lead to François Mitterrand's presidential victory in 1981. With it, Rimbaud was consecrated as the young, rebel poet of the left.

As had been the case in 1954, the year of the centenary of the poet's birth, there was no shortage of commemorative activities in 1991, one hundred years after Rimbaud's death. The socialist government led the way: Mitterrand's minister of culture, Jack Lang, asked people to send a poem of Rimbaud's to two people, each of whom would in turn send one of his poems to another two people: the exponentially expanding Rimbaud mail chain would quickly spread around the world. When asked if the government actually read the poet, Lang responded by asking who in government had *not* wanted to 'change life'; he then explained that if they didn't

David Wojnarowicz, from *Arthur Rimbaud in New York*, Gelatin silver print on paper, 1978–9.

read him, they soon would: he had sent everyone in his government 'Éternité' to start the mail chain.

Rimbaud's life and work have remained constant sources of inspiration for visual artists, who have also come up with their share of answers. David Wojnarowicz put a Rimbaud mask (from the famous Carjat photograph) on models for *Arthur Rimbaud in New York*, 1978–9, his series on the pre-AIDS gay scene in New York. The anachronistic jolt of seeing Rimbaud's face in Coney Island or riding the New York Subway is counterbalanced by the modernity that the face announces; in similar ways, the photo's depictions of drug use and sexual intimacy are somehow, strangely, not out of place, despite their displacement in time and space. Similarly jarring, and successful, was the work that same year by Ernest Pignon-Ernest's series of life-size posters with the poet's face atop a body dressed in clothing that would befit a contemporary vagabond; plastered throughout Charleville and Paris in particular, their reminder of Rimbaud's modern urban experience was also both out of place and apposite.

The poet is memorialized throughout the performing arts, from Benjamin Britten's cycle *Les Illuminations* (1940, which begins with the famous final line from 'Parade') to Christopher Hampton's play of 1967, which helped launch his own career and led to the full-length motion picture *Total Eclipse* (1995), for which Hampton wrote the screenplay. In addition to Jim Morrison, a seemingly endless list of singers have drawn their inspiration from Rimbaud's life and work, including most notably Bob Dylan, Léo Ferré, Serge Gainsbourg and Van Morrison. No doubt the most fervent among them is Patti Smith, who at the age of sixteen discovered a kindred spirit while reading a translation of *Illuminations* in a Philadelphia bus depot. In her albums and poems alike he is a recurring presence, a sort of travelling companion: examples include the song 'Land: Horses/Land of a Thousand Dances/La Mer (de)' from her debut studio album *Horses* (1975); the two live tracks 'Radio Ethiopia' and 'Abyssinia' from her

Ernest Pignon-Ernest, *Rimbaud, à Paris*, 1978.

second album, *Radio Ethiopia* (1976); and the title song from her third album, *Easter* (1978), in which she infuses her music with references to Rimbaud's life and quotations from his poems.[6]

Despite this relentless stream of answers, Rimbaud's questions persist. He answered them, time and time again; unable to accept his answers, we keep looking for new ones. Surely he provided an answer in his poem 'Départ', from *Illuminations* (OC, 296):

Assez vu. La vision s'est rencontrée à tous les airs.
Assez eu. Rumeurs des villes, le soir, et au soleil, et toujours.
Assez connu. Les arrêts de la vie. – Ô rumeurs et Visions!
Départ dans l'affection et le bruit neufs!

Seen enough. The vision met itself in every kind of air. / Had enough. Noises of cities in the evening, in the sunlight, and forever. / Known enough. The haltings of life. – Oh! Noises and Visions! / Departure into new affection and sound!

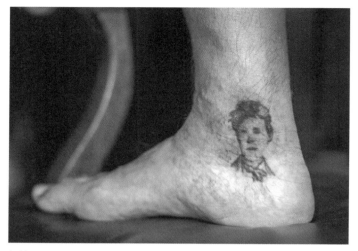

Ankle tattoo.

Our inability to grasp Rimbaud's answers comes from the fact that he calls for us to leave precisely when we want to stay and linger. We want him to give more at the moment when he has nothing left to give. But what he gave us – what he left us – does indeed keep on giving. Through the poems that provide more questions than answers, through his erratic itinerary, and through the brilliant irreverence and irreverent brilliance that holds it all together, there will always be enough Rimbaud for all of us.

References

1 Walls

1 *oc*, 338, 355, 363 and 370, respectively.
2 It would be soon interrupted by the end of the Franco-Prussian War and the Paris Commune and appear as a volume in 1871; the third and final volume of the series was published only as a volume, in 1876.
3 This, too, is more copying: again, Victor Hugo is in the mix. For Hugo himself had already produced a similar rhyme in his poem 'À des oiseaux envolés' (To Flown-off Birds), from his 1837 collection *Les Voix intérieures*: 'Ce livre des oiseaux et des bohémiens, / Ce poème de Dieu qui vaut mieux que les miens' (This book of birds and bohemians, / This poem of God that is worth more than my own), a pair of rhymes so important that Banville quoted it in his *Petit traité de poésie française*. In Hugo's poem, the bohemian split 'bo-hé-mi-ens' is sewn up by 'Ce poème de Dieu', which restores order and unity, resulting first in the echo 'mi' in 'mieux' and then culminating in the 'miens' at the end of the line. In Rimbaud's 'Sensation', on the other hand, nothing is reified. To the contrary: the absolute negation of 'je ne penserai rien' leads to the breakdown of subjectivity in 'mi-en' and reveals Banville's blind spot; while he explicitly evokes 'mien', 'rien' and 'bohémien' in his rule, he misses the portmanteau words that lurk within, when 'mien' is not a standalone word but hidden elsewhere. Therein lies part of what Rimbaud is getting at: that part of subjectivity that is not asserted as such, but rather exists *within* other states (such as being 'bo-hé-mi-ens'). So whereas Hugo's rhyme stretches out 'bo-hé-mi-ens' and ends with unity and concision, Rimbaud's move goes in the opposite direction, and the combination of rhyme and synaeresis

places additional emphasis on the destabilized subjectivity – the 'mien', no longer unified but slowly pulled apart – that Rimbaud's poetry brings to the lyric.

4   The present bust is the third, sitting there since October 1954; the first one, created by Rimbaud's posthumous brother-in-law Paterne Berrichon, was inaugurated in 1901, and a second one, by Alphonse Colle, was put in its place in 1927. Both times, the poet Gustave Kahn spoke at the inauguration, and both times, the statue disappeared during the German occupation of the city during a World War.

5   He would later attempt another series of prose poems, under the collective title *Les Déserts de l'amour* (most likely in 1871): 'Avertissement', 'C'est certes la même campagne [. . .]' and 'Cette fois, c'est la Femme [. . .]'.

2 Fields

1   It is hard to overstate the importance of Demeny's inactivity. If he had done what Rimbaud had asked and burned the manuscripts, thirteen poems would have been lost for good, as no other versions remain: 'Morts de '92 . . .', 'Roman', 'Rêvé pour l'hiver', 'Le Buffet', 'L'Éclatante Victoire de Sarrebrück', 'La Maline', 'Au Cabaret-Vert', 'Le Dormeur du val', 'Bal des pendus', 'Le Châtiment de Tartufe', 'Ma Bohême', 'Le Mal' and 'Rages de Césars'. Demeny would eventually sell the manuscripts to Rimbaud's early biographer Rodolphe Darzens, and they would be bought and sold by collectors until Stefan Zweig purchased them at auction, at which point they joined what would later be called the Stefan Zweig Collection, housed at the British Library since the 1980s. For more on the *recueil Demeny* see *OC1*, pp. 149–60. Rimbaud would continue to send poems to Demeny: 'Chant de guerre parisien', 'Mes petites amoureuses', 'Accroupissements', 'Les Poètes de sept ans' and 'Les Pauvres à l'église' are other poems that only exist today because Demeny saved the manuscripts.

2   'Nos Peintres au Champ-de-Mars', *La Situation*, 1 July 1867.

3   *OC*, 337–8. The term 'sans-cœur' (heartless) comes from Hugo: 'Ce que dit la bouche d'ombre' (What the mouth of darkness says), the poem

in *Les Contemplations* from which Rimbaud borrowed the title for a term he used for his mother.

3 Capital

1 The pun comes from the paronomasia between 'on me pense' (people think me) and 'on me panse' (people groom me).
2 The French verb *voler* means both to steal and to fly. Both are supported here: the former through the obvious reference to Proudhon's famous slogan 'La propriété, c'est le vol' (property is theft), and the latter because caricatures of the period commonly portrayed the reactionary Republican leaders as insects.
3 See Kristin Rars, *The Emergence of Social Space: Rimbaud and the Paris Commune* (Minneapolis, MN, 1988; revd edn London, 2008).
4 Stéphane Mallarmé, 'Arthur Rimbaud', *The Chap-book*, 15 May 1906, pp. 8, 10.
5 The Vilains Bonshommes had had an album, too, although it went up in smoke during the burning of the Hôtel de Ville; either Verlaine or Valade – both of whom had office jobs leading up to the Commune – had left it in a desk at work.
6 The poems are 'Les Assis', 'Les Chercheuses de poux', 'L'Homme juste', 'Tête de faune', 'Le Cœur volé', 'Les Mains de Jeanne-Marie', 'Les Effarés', 'Les Voyelles', 'L'étoile a pleuré rose [. . .]', 'Les Douaniers', 'Oraison du soir', 'Les Sœurs de Charité' and 'Les Premières Communions'. See *oc1*, 349–74.

4 Cities

1 Ex-Madame Paul Verlaine, *Mémoires de ma vie*, ed. Michael Pakenham (Seyssel, 1992), p. 162.
2 Although divorce was authorized in 1792, modified by decrees in 1793 and 1794, and included in Napoleon's 1804 Code civil, it was abrogated under the Restoration in 1816 and would only be re-established under the Third Republic with the loi Naquet of 1884.

3 Quoted in Auguste Martin, *Verlaine et Rimbaud: Documents inédits tires des Archives de la Préfecture de Police* (Paris, 1943), pp. 10–12.

4 Paul Verlaine, 'Notes on England: Myself as a French Master', *The Fortnightly Review*, July 1894.

5 On 14 October 1883, Delahaye sent Verlaine a letter with two sonnets that are Zutique in tone: entitled 'Les anciens animaux . . .' and 'Nos fesses ne sont pas les leurs . . .', they were first published by the editor Albert Messein in 1923, with 'Sonnet du trou du cul' under the title *Stupra* (Obscenities).

6 Rimbaud criticism has not tired in its attempts to find her, concluding that 'H' stands for the guillotine, masturbation, homosexuality, hashish and time, among many others; see *oc*, 978–9.

7 German troops used the house as their *Kommandantur* during the First World War and blew it up when they left; all that is left of the original structure is the side of one wall. The site, including the house that was built where the farm used to be, was saved from ruin and purchased by Patti Smith in 2017.

5 Wounds

1 When his mother asked him what *Une saison en enfer* was about, he simply replied that it meant what it says: 'littéralement et dans tous les sens' (literally and in all directions/senses). Isabelle Rimbaud, *Reliques*, 2nd edn (Paris, 1921), p. 143.

2 *De profundis Domine* is short for *De profundis clamavi ad te, Domine* (Out of the depths I have cried to thee, O Lord), the first line of Psalm 130 of the Penitential Psalms.

3 For more on this delirium that is an un-reading – a reading against the grain of typical reading (thus a kind of madness that makes poetry un-readable) – see Shoshana Felman, *La Folie et la chose littéraire* (Paris, 1978), pp. 108–9.

4 On the recto of some of the manuscripts from *Une saison en enfer* figure parodic texts commonly referred to as 'Proses dites "évangéliques"'; seemingly of the same period as the composition of the *Saison*, these three prose texts, inspired by the Gospel of John, portray Christ and his miracles as ineffective.

5　Losseau had copies sent to friends, including Maurice Maeterlinck, Émile Verhaeren and Stefan Zweig. Losseau went so far as to publish a pamphlet denouncing Isabelle's account, first in the 1915 annual report of the Société des bibliophiles et iconophiles de Belgique and then as a standalone pamphlet the following year.

6　See Vernon P. Underwood, 'Rimbaud anglicisant', *Revue de littérature comparée*, xxxvi/3 (1 July 1962), pp. 337–8.

6 Worlds

1　*Ninety-three* is a novel by Victor Hugo, published in 1874.

2　According to Delahaye, Rimbaud arrived in Vienna without money or resources, lived as a vagrant for a few days, got into a fight with a policeman and was brought to the border. There, German officials deemed him unwelcome and brought him to the border with Alsace, to return on foot to Charleville.

3　Rimbaud's Alpine trek also anticipates the route currently taken by refugees wishing to avoid the official crossing from Italy into France.

4　The remaining one, a self-portrait, is in the Bibliothèque nationale de France.

5　The images in the collection of the Musée Rimbaud are so light that they cannot be reproduced with accuracy in publications. Versions of the photos that do appear distort contrast and other elements in order to produce a visible image, but the distortion is too great to justify their inclusion here. For more on these images in all their variations, see Jean-Jacques Lefrère, *Face à Rimbaud* (Paris, 2006), as well as the studies by the bibliophile Jacques Desse of les Libraires associés.

6　It would grow into a two-part series, with profiles of Tristan Corbière, Rimbaud and Mallarmé published by Léon Vanier in 1884, and three more profiles – of Marceline Desbordes-Valmore, Villiers de l'Isle-Adam, and of Verlaine himself under the anagram 'Pauvre Lelian' – added to a second edition for 1888.

7　In issue 5 (13 May 1886), *La Vogue* published 'Après le Déluge', 'Enfance', 'Conte', 'Parade', 'Antique', 'Being Beauteous', 'Ô la face cendrée [. . .]', 'Vies', 'Départ', 'Royauté', 'À une Raison', 'Matinée d'ivresse', 'Phrases', 'Ouvriers', 'Les Ponts', 'Ville' and 'Ornières', all from *Illuminations*; issue 6 (29 May): 'Villes' ('Ce sont des villes! [. . .])', 'Vagabonds', 'Villes' ('L'acropole officielle [. . .])', 'Veillées', 'Mystique', 'Aube', 'Fleurs', 'Nocturne vulgaire', 'Marine', 'Fête d'hiver', 'Angoisse', 'Métropolitain' and 'Barbare'. In issue 7 (7 June), the verse poems 'Chanson de la plus haute Tour', 'Âge d'or', '"Nous sommes tes grands-parents . . ."' ('Comédie de la soif'), 'Éternité' and '"Qu'est-ce pour nous, mon cœur . . ."' Finally a combination of poems from *Illuminations* and verse poems in issues 8 (13 June): 'Promontoire', 'Scènes', 'Soir historique', 'Michel et Christine', 'Juillet', 'Honte'; and 9 (21 June): 'Mouvement', 'Bottom', 'H', 'Dévotion', 'Démocratie', 'Loin des oiseaux [. . .]' ('Larme'), 'Ô saisons, ô châteaux [. . .]' and 'La Rivière de Cassis'.

8   Letter from Armand Savouré to Georges Maurevert, 3 April 1930, published in *L'Éclaireur de Nice*, quoted in JJL, p. 1048.

9   Isabelle Rimbaud, *Reliques*, 3rd edn (Paris, 1921), pp. 65–9.

7 Afterlives

1   Henry Miller, *The Time of the Assassins: A Study of Rimbaud* [1946] (New York, 1962), p. 6.

2   See Adrianna M. Paliyenko, *Mis-reading the Creative Impulse: The Poetic Subject in Rimbaud and Claudel, Restaged* (Carbondale, IL, 1997).

3   Bouillane de Lacoste produced a critical edition of the verse poems (*Poésies*) in 1939, a second edition in 1947 and, in 1949, two volumes devoted to *Illuminations* (a study and an edition). The Pléiade edition of Rimbaud would also be re-edited, each time revised and with new content, in 1963, 1972 and 2009.

4   See Bruce Morrissette, *The Great Rimbaud Forgery: The Affair of 'La Chasse spirituelle'* (Saint Louis, MO, 1956).

5   The Maoist group Vive la révolution! (VLR) led by Roland Castro and Tiennot Grumbach used this phrase in the title of its *Changer la vie: document politique* (Kremlin-Bicêtre, 1970).

6   See Carrie Noland, 'Rimbaud and Patti Smith: The Discoveries of Modern Poetry and the Popular Music Industry', in *Poetry at Stake: Lyric Aesthetics and the Challenge of Technology* (Princeton, NJ, 1999), pp. 163–84.

Bibliography

Works by Rimbaud

Un concert d'enfers: vies et poésies [Rimbaud and Verlaine], ed. Solenn Dupas, Yann Frémy and Henri Scepi (Paris, 2017)

Correspondance, ed. Jean-Jacques Lefrère (Paris, 2007)

Œuvres. I: Poésies. II: Une saison en enfer, Vers nouveaux. III: Illuminations, Correspondance, ed. Jean-Luc Steinmetz (Paris, 1989)

Œuvres complètes, ed. Pierre Brunel (Paris, 1999)

Œuvres complètes, ed. André Guyaux and Aurélia Cervoni (Paris, 2009)

Œuvres complètes, ed. Steve Murphy (vol. I: *Poésies*, 1999; vol. II: *Œuvres diverses et lettres 1864/1865–1870*, 2007; vol. IV: *Fac-similés*, 2002)

Poésies, Une saison en enfer, Illuminations, ed. Dominique Combe (Paris, 2004)

Works by Rimbaud in English translation

Complete Works, Selected Letters, trans. Wallace Fowlie, revd and with a new introduction by Seth Whidden (Chicago, IL, 2005)

I Promise to be Good: The Letters of Arthur Rimbaud, trans. Wyatt Mason (New York, 2003)

Rimbaud Complete, trans. Wyatt Mason (New York, 2002)

Selected Poems and Letters, trans. John Sturrock and Jeremy Harding (London, 2004)

Works on Rimbaud

Ahearn, Edward J., *Rimbaud: Visions and Habitations* (Berkeley, CA, 1983)

Berger, Anne-Emmanuelle, *Le Banquet de Rimbaud: recherches sur l'oralité* (Seyssel, 1992)

Bobillot, Jean-Pierre, *Rimbaud, le meurtre d'Orphée: Crise de Verbe & chimie des vers ou la Commune dans le Poëme* (Paris, 2004)

Borer, Alain, *Rimbaud en Abyssinie* (Paris, 1984), trans. Rosmarie Waldrop as *Rimbaud in Abyssinia* (New York, 1991)

—, *Rimbaud d'Arabie* (Paris, 1991)

Bourguignon, Jean, and Charles Houin, *Vie d'Arthur Rimbaud* [1901], ed. Michel Drouin (Paris, 1991)

Brunel, Pierre, *Arthur Rimbaud, ou l'éclatant désastre* (Seyssel, 1983)

—, *Rimbaud, Projets et réalisations* (Paris, 1983)

Claisse, Bruno, *'Les Illuminations' et l'accession au réel* (Paris, 2012)

—, *Rimbaud, ou 'le dégagement rêvé': essai sur l'idéologie des 'Illuminations'* (Charleville-Mézières, 1990)

Cornulier, Benoît de, *De la métrique à l'interprétation: essais sur Rimbaud* (Paris, 2009)

Fongaro, Antoine, *Rimbaud: texte, sens et interprétations* (Toulouse, 1994)

Fowlie, Wallace, *Rimbaud and Jim Morrison: The Rebel as Poet* (Durham, NC, 1993)

Frémy, Yann, *'Te voilà, c'est la force': essai sur 'Une saison en enfer' de Rimbaud* (Paris, 2009)

Guyaux, André, *Poétique du fragment: essai sur les 'Illuminations'* (Neuchâtel, 1985)

Izambard, Georges, *Rimbaud tel que je l'ai connu* (Paris, 1963)

Lawler, James, *Rimbaud's Theatre of the Self* (Cambridge, MA, 1992)

Lefrère, Jean-Jacques, *Arthur Rimbaud* (Paris, 2001)

Matucci, Mario, *Le Dernier Visage de Rimbaud en Afrique: d'après des documents inédits* (Paris, 1962)

Murat, Michel, *L'Art de Rimbaud* (Paris, 2002; revd edn 2013)

Murphy, Steve, *Le Premier Rimbaud, ou l'apprentissage de la subversion* (Paris and Lyon, 1990)

—, *Rimbaud et la Commune: microlectures et perspectives* (Paris, 2010)

—, *Stratégies de Rimbaud* (Paris, 2004; revd edn 2009)

Nakaji, Yoshikazu, *Combat spirituel ou immense dérision? essai d'analyse textuelle d'"Une saison en enfer'* (Paris, 1987)

Nicholl, Charles, *Somebody Else: Arthur Rimbaud in Africa, 1880–1891* (London, 1997)

Parade sauvage: revue d'études rimbaldiennes [journal], 1984–present

Petitfils, Pierre, *Rimbaud* (Paris, 1982), trans. Alan Sheridan (Charlottesville, va, 1988)

Reboul, Yves, *Rimbaud dans son temps* (Paris, 2009)

Robb, Graham, *Rimbaud: A Biography* (London, 2000)

Ross, Kristin, *The Emergence of Social Space: Rimbaud and the Paris Commune* (Minneapolis, mn, 1988; revd edn London, 2008)

Sacchi, Sergio, *Études sur 'Les Illuminations' de Rimbaud* (Paris, 2002)

Saint-Amand, Denis, *La Littérature à l'ombre: sociologie du zutisme* (Paris, 2012)

St Clair, Robert, *Poetry, Politics, and the Body in Rimbaud: Lyrical Material* (Oxford, 2018)

Scott, Clive, *Translating Rimbaud's 'Illuminations'* (Exeter, 2006)

Steinmetz, Jean-Luc, *Arthur Rimbaud: une question de presence* (Paris, 1991), trans. Jon Graham as *Arthur Rimbaud: Presence of an Enigma* (New York, 2002)

Teyssèdre, Bernard, *Arthur Rimbaud et le foutoir zutique* (Paris, 2011)

Verlaine, Ex-Madame Paul, *Mémoires de ma vie*, ed. Michael Pakenham (Seyssel, 1992)

Whidden, Seth, *Leaving Parnassus: The Lyric Subject in Verlaine and Rimbaud* (Amsterdam, 2007)

—, ed., *La Poésie jubilatoire: Rimbaud, Verlaine et l'"Album zutique'* (Paris, 2010)

White, Edmund, *Rimbaud: The Double Life of a Rebel* (London, 2009)

Acknowledgements

My debt to earlier studies of poets, their work, and their milieu is considerable. Indeed, what is a great challenge is an equally great pleasure: taking stock of everything already written and forging ahead in a manner that is compelling. The present study rests on the shoulders of giants who left us too soon: Ross Chambers (1932–2017), Jean-Jacques Lefrère (1954–2015) and Michael Pakenham (1929–2013). Different in many ways, each had a relentless curiosity and persistent drive to add to already encyclopaedic knowledge, and each showed – time and time again – how biography and criticism remain so intertwined. Just as important, each had a natural generosity and undeniable personal warmth. In gratitude for all that they shared with me, I dedicate this book to their memory.

This study's interpretations of Rimbaud's poetry rely on beliefs commonly held by most scholars today. As they flip through these pages, many fellow *rimbaldiens* will recognize their fingerprints. I am particularly grateful for the most indelible smudges, which come from Steve Murphy: over the last thirty years no one has contributed more erudition or *générosité d'esprit* to Rimbaud studies. I am fortunate to have benefited immensely from both, as well as from his friendship. Similar thanks for shaping my thoughts on Rimbaud are due to Edward Ahearn, Yann Frémy, the late Dennis Minahen and Robert St. Clair.

Vivian Constantinopoulos first contacted me about this book and remained patient until my schedule allowed me to write it; I am grateful for her sustained support and hope that she feels it was worth the wait. She and the entire Reaktion team have been a pleasure to work with from start to finish. For their assistance with illustrations and archival material, I wish to thank Laetitia Dehoul of the Musée Rimbaud and Élise

Nicolas of the Médiathèque Voyelles, both in Charleville-Mézières. Many visitors to the city will naturally step foot inside the Vieux Moulin, site of the museum; that the Médiathèque should be housed in the library that was the inspiration for 'Les Assis' – where a certain adolescent was a near permanent fixture and an equally frequent thorn in the side of librarian and future historian Jean Hubert, who disapproved of the young patron's book requests – makes it all the more fitting. Thanks, finally, to Jacques Desse of Les Libraires associés for his assistance with my iconographical queries.

Photo Acknowledgements

The author and the publishers wish to express their thanks to the below sources of illustrative material and / or permission to reproduce it:

Bibliothèque nationale de France / Réunion des musées nationaux, Paris: pp. 160, 175; Jacques Desse (crédit Libraires associés / Adoc photos): p. 156; Médiathèque Voyelles: pp. 8, 15, 19, 29, 36, 49, 55, 59, 85, 90, 138, 156, 168, 171, 172; Musée Arthur Rimbaud, Charleville-Mézières: pp. 20, 33, 157, 165 (Bardey family documents), 178; Musée d'Orsay / Réunion des musées nationaux, Paris: p. 92; Ernest Pignon-Ernest: pp. 180, 189; private collection: pp. 176, 185, 190 (photo David Olds); Courtesy of the Estate of David Wojnarowicz and P•P•O•W, New York, copyright © Estate of David Wojnarowicz: p. 187.